MASTERING THE ART OF

Florida Seafood

LONNIE T. LYNCH

PINEAPPLE PRESS, INC.
Sarasota, Florida

Disclaimer

Please use caution in the kitchen and buy fresh seafood from a reputable source. Neither the author nor the publisher will assume responsibility for any illness contracted after eating seafood used in these recipes.

Inquiries should be addressed to:
Pineapple Press, Inc.
P.O. Box 3899
Sarasota, FL 34230

www.pineapplepress.com

Library of Congress Cataloging-in-Publication Data

Lynch, Lonnie T., 1960–
        Mastering the art of Florida seafood / Lonnie T. Lynch. — 1st ed.
                p.   cm.
        ISBN 1-56164-176-6 (alk. paper)
        1. Cookery (Seafood) 2. Cookery—Florida. I. Title.
    TX747.L88   1999
    641.6'92'09759—dc21   99-26592
                                                                    CIP

First Edition
10 9 8 7 6 5 4 3 2 1

Design by Osprey Design Systems
Printed by Versa Press, East Peoria, Illinois

To my mother, Joyce D. Agee, I would like to give special thanks.

Special recognition to Bob Barry, my good friend always. I could not have done these projects without your valuable help and guidance.

I would like to thank George Galluzi for sharing his famous saying, "Don't be a jack of all trades. Be a specialist of one."

Table of Contents

Welcome to Cooking Florida Seafood

As a professional chef in Palm Beach County, I have put together a variety of seafood dishes that can easily be created and enjoyed by all. Cooking seafood should be enjoyable and fun. Both this book and my career in cooking are based on my beliefs that being good at cooking and entertaining is only a matter of having confidence and enjoying what you are doing.

Florida is blessed with an abundance of fresh seafood such as dolphin, stone crab, alligator, and yellow tail. In this cookbook we will use native seafood, as well as imported varieties such as salmon, oysters, clams, and other delicacies.

There are many myths on how to cook seafood. To me, cooking requires fresh ingredients, good sauces, and a lot of imagination. You can use this book to create some impressive meals for your guests after discovering here the diversity and delicacy of more than one hundred recipes that have been used professionally.

While in Florida, I have had the opportunity to work at many fine restaurants, hotels, and country clubs, creating and serving many seafood dishes. I have been fortunate to work with many classy chefs and cooks that have helped to inspire the creative ideas that make Florida cooking and cuisine a treasury in itself. Florida is blessed with various cultures and an influx of regional chefs and cooks, which have all blended together to create a uniquely different cuisine, a product of diverse culinary influences.

Even though these recipes have been used in gourmet restaurants, I have tried to include a variety of recipes that you can create at home. The recipes are arranged from the easiest to the more difficult, so if you are unfamiliar with cooking with seafood, you can start with the easier

> While cooking, have fun and be creative. And most of all, enjoy yourself! Thank you, Florida, and your uniquely diverse culture, for offering many approaches to preparing seafood—all delicious, all Floridian.

recipes and continue on to the harder ones as your skill and confidence grows.

One of the most interesting aspects of Florida cooking is its imaginative use of different ingredients and its unusual combination of ingredients. With its borders surrounded by Cajun country, the South, and the Caribbean, Florida is filled with ideas and inspirations that create a culinary hotbed.

Be creative! Many of the sauces and recipes used in specific seafood dishes may be used individually to create exciting new recipes and ideas.

Understanding and Preparing Seafood

Seafood—The Healthy Choice

Food and nutrition have taken on greater significance in the health revolution. Your diet will help shape your future health! A meal planned around seafood is high in protein and low in fat, which experts say makes it a healthier choice than meals dominated by meat. The edible part of fish normally has fifteen to twenty percent protein. Fish protein is excellent nutrition because it contains most of the essential amino acids, and its fat is polyunsaturated. Fresh fish is one of the most wholesome, nutritious, and delicious foods you can eat. Shellfish are also a very tasty source of protein.

The six basic nutrients are proteins, fats, carbohydrates, vitamins, minerals, and water. Nutrients are what the body needs to maintain life. The body converts protein, carbohydrates, and fats into energy. Vitamins and minerals in themselves supply no energy but assist the body's metabolism. As a rule, protein and carbohydrates have four calories per gram; fat has nine calories per gram.

When using these recipes, feel free to make adjustments to meet your dietary needs. You can replace heavy cream with skim milk or lactated milk as necessary. Use lighter oils when possible, and use smaller portions and add more vegetables to suit your taste.

If you're like me, eating more seafood and less junk food is a delicious and appetizing way to enjoy a healthy diet. In short, we can and should choose how we live and how we eat.

Seafood's variety runs as deep as the water in which it swims and is generally a source of great nutrition. Almost all fish deliver high-quality, easily digestible protein with a minimum of saturated fat, LDL-cholesterol, and calories. When it comes to fish, most of the fat it contains is polyunsaturated, rather than saturated fat associated with red meat. Some types of fish contain almost no fat at all.

Fish and shellfish are also good sources of the B vitamins, including B6 and B12, niacin, and biotin. The dietary minerals potassium and iron, which the body needs in fairly large amounts, are also supplied by seafood, and marine foods are generally the main source of iodine in our diets. They're also an excellent source of the trace minerals zinc and selenium.

Shellfish are high in protein, calcium, riboflavin, and niacin. They may contain as much as three percent fat and provide only small amounts of carbohydrate. But, shellfish are high in cholesterol! Lobster has twice as much cholesterol as meat but may prove worth the treat.

Lean fish is an excellent source of protein and has little fat. Seven ounces of white fish contain only about 160 calories. Examples of lean fish are sole, sea bass, haddock, and trout.

Oily fish contain more fat than lean fish, but the amount varies—seven ounces of oily fish contain about four hundred calories. Examples of oily fish are salmon, mackerel, eel, and sardines.

4

Types of Seafood

Alligator

A genus of the crocodile family, alligator is found in the Gulf states and swamplands. Alligator meat is available at some Florida markets and restaurants, and it comes in three types: belly meat, which is tender, white, and veal-like; body meat, which has a slightly tougher texture and is pinkish, with a strong flavor; and tail meat, which is dark in color and used only in braised dishes because it is often tough.

Calamari (Squid)

Squid is a member of the mollusk family and has a firm, chewy texture and mildly sweet flavor. A cephalopod, it is related to the octopus and cuttlefish. Cooking should always be brief since squid becomes tough and rubbery when overdone. The liquid in the ink sacs may be extracted and used for color preparations in pasta or other favorite dishes. Squid is rich in both protein and phosphorus.

Clams

Clams are bivalves and have an edible flesh inside of two hinged shells. Atlantic clams range in size from Little Necks (which are the smallest and most tender) and small soft-shell steamers to Cherrystones and large chowder clams.

Chowder clams are used for soup, and most of the other varieties are served on the half shell, either raw or steamed with wine and garlic. For soup or pasta, you can purchase canned or frozen preshucked clams.

Clams are available year-round but are best in the colder months. When purchasing live clams, select only those that are tightly shut or will close when touched! Scrub clam shells well before cooking.

Conch (pronounced "konk")

Conch are versatile univalves that are excellent in salads, soups, and entrées. Conch flesh is tough but may be tenderized by long, slow cooking or by pounding with a mallet. Conch meat may also be ground, added to a batter, and deep fried to make delicious conch fritters.

Conch is available year-round and is harvested off both coasts of Florida. Conch should have a sweet flavor, never too fishy!

Crab

These crustaceans are harvested from both the Atlantic and Pacific Oceans as well the Gulf of Mexico.

Dungeness and blue crab have edible meat in the body and claw. In the Alaskan king crab and spider crab, the edible meat is in the legs and claws. Soft-shell blue crabs that have just molted their hard shells are entirely edible.

In case you've never tried them, stone crab claws are a special Florida treat! The only edible meat in stone crabs is inside the claws. They are available in Florida only during the winter months, unless imported.

When shopping, choose crabmeat that will correspond with the way you intend to serve it. Price often is a major factor—the most expensive is lump crabmeat. Live crabs should still be kicking and not sluggish.

Lobster

In Florida, we usually eat two types of these crustaceans. Florida, or spiny, lobster contains edible meat in the tail only and is found in Florida and Caribbean waters as well as off the coast of California. Maine lobster is found off the Atlantic coast from Labrador to Virginia and has edible meat in the tail as well as each claw.

Cooked lobster can be eaten hot, or cold, as in a salad. The lobster shell turns bright red when cooked. Split cooked lobsters by turning them over and cutting them in half lengthwise with a French knife. (See page 78, Splitting Whole Lobsters.)

Mussels

Mussels are found attached to rocks on the Atlantic and Pacific Coasts. They have a smooth, blue-black shell with deep yellow or orange flesh. East Coast mussels are sold fresh year-round, while West Coast mussels are fresh only during the winter months.

Mussels should only be purchased live or precooked. Avoid any that are open and check for a sweet smell. Scrub mussels with a brush to remove the "beard" on the shells before cooking. Mussels can be purchased preshucked in buckets and are also available frozen in half-shells.

Oysters

Oysters live in shallow, temperate waters. Most varieties are available year-round, but oysters are sweetest during the winter months. When purchasing oysters, they should be either alive, preshucked, in jars, or smoked and packed in tins. Fresh oysters should have their shells tightly closed when handled—this signifies that they are alive.

Scallops

Scallops are found off both the Atlantic and Gulf Coasts. The sweet edible part is the muscle that holds the shell together. Sea scallops are about half- to one-inch thick. Bay scallops are much smaller. Both varieties are available all year. Frozen scallops are available year-round.

Shrimp

Shrimp or prawn? The debate on the terminology has been brewing for years. What we can say is that shrimp live in salt water and prawn are found in fresh water. The word "prawn" is used commercially for large shrimp.

Shrimp come in brown, white, and pink varieties. Both cooked and raw shrimp should feel firm and smell sweet. Removal of the black intestinal vein (deveining) should be done on all shrimp before you eat them. (See page 119, How to Clean and Butterfly Shrimp.)

Most fish markets carry both cooked and uncooked shrimp, which usually have been frozen and thawed before reselling.

Flat Fish vs. Round Fish

With the wide variety of fish available, here are a couple of purchasing tips. Fish are generally classified into two categories—round fish and flat fish. Round fish can be cooked whole or cut off the bone into either steaks or two fillets; examples are salmon, dolphin, and snapper. Flat fish, such as sole and flounder, are cut into fillets.

Fish are also classified as either lean or oily. Lean fish have a milder flavor and firm, white flesh. Snapper, sole, and halibut are examples of lean fish. Oily fish are stronger in flavor and darker in color than lean fish. Examples are swordfish, salmon, trout, and catfish.

When choosing an entrée to prepare, always try to consider the size and the flavor of the fish you will be serving.

Purchasing and Preparing Seafood

Purchasing and preparing seafood are the subjects of many books. Here we will simply go over some hints and tips that you, as a consumer, will find extremely valuable.

You should purchase your seafood from a reputable store or dealer, for it has a short shelf life. Lakes, rivers, and oceans are full of hundreds of species of delicious seafood. Today, seafood is shipped from all over the world, but it is extremely perishable and should be treated accordingly. Fresh seafood is always the best way to go, and it can be purchased at a pier market. Seafood is also available frozen, with the best selection found at specialty fish markets.

Deciding whether fresh or frozen seafood should be used is entirely up to you. In any event, seafood should not smell too fishy—this is a sure sign of age or improper handling by the fishmonger or store.

If seafood at the store was previously frozen, ask the salesperson how long has it been thawed and take the time to handpick it. Always use the freshest possible seafood to create the best possible dish.

Don't expose seafood to excessive heat for any length of time. Doing this will undoubtedly lead to the meat being overcooked and somewhat tough by losing its moisture. Cook seafood only until the flesh turns opaque.

Fresh fish is the secret to delicious seafood recipes. (The second secret is not to overcook.)

Seafood should be thoroughly cleaned, with all skin and scales removed, unless it is being cooked whole. Fish should always be gutted as soon as possible, ideally at the moment it is caught.

When purchasing fresh fish, always get it deboned and skinned if possible.

Herbs and Spices

Herbs

Herbs are used both to conjure up extra flavor in your dishes and to add color. To use herbs properly, add just a pinch at a time. Herbs should be added to dishes near the end of cooking time in order to retain their flavor. Do not be afraid to experiment with your favorite herbs or to create your own exciting combinations.

Parsley and chives can be used in quantity without overly altering the flavor of the dish. They can also add a nice splash of color to the dish if placed just before serving.

Spices

The history of spices extends back four thousand years. Spices originated in the Far East and have been historically valued for their aroma and flavor. As a household chef, you should always have on hand a fresh selection of your favorite herbs and spices to enhance the flavor of your dishes. When possible, buy whole spices that can be ground just before use, as this will preserve their flavor. Spices should never overpower the natural flavor of the food, they should enhance it—so be sure to use them sparingly. Store spices in tightly covered containers in a cool, dark place.

A Selection of Herbs and Spices

Fresh herbs and spices will add a wonderful zest of flavor that will have your palette jumping.

A selection of herbs and spices useful in seafood preparation follows:
Bay Leaves
Chervil
Chives
Cilantro
Coriander

Dill
Fennel
Lemon Thyme
Marjoram
Mint
Opal Basil
Oregano
Parsley
Rosemary
Sage
Savory
Sorrel
Sweet Basil
Tarragon
Thyme

Seasonings

Seasonings are added to food to intensify or improve its flavor. When preparing seafood, various condiments, sauces, relishes, and seasonings are frequently used. When using condiments to flavor sauces and seafood, use moderate amounts at first so as not to over-flavor. Certain specialty gourmet products on the market, such as chutneys, salsas, and hot sauces, can be fun to experiment with when cooking different dishes.

Specialty Seasonings

Specialty nuts and seeds, fresh ginger, leeks, onions, shallots, garlic, horseradish, and mustards are used for flavoring. Specialty grains, meals, flours and other starches are used for breading and adding subtle flavors. Garlic and shallots are little bulbs of treasure that will add flavor to many dishes.

Here are just a few general hints and tips. Consult individual recipes for details.

Specialty Oils

Use of the following oils can help accentuate the flavors of your dishes: canola, coconut, corn, cottonseed, grapeseed, olive, peanut, safflower, salad, sesame, soybean, sunflower, walnut, and vegetable. Great chefs always use only the finest oil, lard, and shortening available. For salads, use only the first pressing of olive and nut oils. Cooking oils should always have a high smoking point so as not to burn at the temperatures necessary for cooking.

Specialty Vinegars

Vinegars are used to introduce sharp, piquant, or sweet flavors into foods. As a household chef, you can create your own specialty vinegars and have a full range on hand for your unique specialty cooking. Balsamic, champagne, malt, raspberry, rice, red wine, sherry, tarragon, and white are just a few of the varieties of vinegars used to add extra flavor to food.

Specialty Condiments

Tabasco, Worcestershire sauce, and Dijon mustard are just a few of the tasty specialty condiments available. You can also try some of the others—such as "Captain Fred's Extra-Special Fish Flavoring"—sold at your local market. Quality of such sauces varies.

Basic Culinary Preparation— The Backbone of the Kitchen

Basic culinary preparations are the backbone of the kitchen. One of the first skills you must master to be efficient in the kitchen is preparation. Preparing your food (chopping, dicing, peeling, and washing) is just as important as the actual cooking. Beautiful preparation equals exquisite presentation.

Every good cook needs to know some basic preparation techniques. A fishmonger can usually cut the seafood and fish, but there are some techniques you will have to master.

Here is where you can find some basic culinary techniques scattered throughout the book:

> Cooking is a lot of washing, chopping, and dicing.

When starting a seafood dish, wash, cut, dice, and slice all the ingredients and set to the side in bowls until ready. When ready to prepare seafood, all the prep will be done and organized.

Cutting vegetables

Vegetable cutting is an art that is almost as important as cooking the food. The way food is cut can affect the cooking method; small pieces will cook faster than large pieces.

Cubing and dicing: Cut vegetables in thick strips, then cut again to form cubes. By cutting a strip only ⅛-inch thick, then cutting into small pieces, you have diced.

Cutting julienne strips: Cut vegetables such as carrots and rutabagas into thin slices; then cut into matchstick strips. Vegetables such as peppers and leeks can be cut in half; lay them out flat and cut into strips. For more details on cutting julienne strips, see page 130.

Chopping onions: Peel onion. Cut in half. Using a sharp knife, make cuts into onion a quarter inch apart. Next cut the opposite way, and the onion should fall apart in a diced cut.

Mincing garlic: Peel garlic and place on a cutting board (peeling is easier if you lightly smash the clove first with the flat of a knife). Cut into small pieces, then mince with a very sharp knife.

Chopping parsley: Wash parsley. Using your hands, roll parsley tight and press flat on cutting board. Using a sharp knife, start cutting parsley into small pieces until you've chopped about halfway down the stem. Chop parsley until fine. Place chopped parsley in the middle of a clean kitchen towel. Grab corners and bring towel together, hold tight, and wash under running water. Squeeze water out and place parsley in bowl for later use. Always save some parsley sprigs for garnish on plates.

Slicing mushrooms: Wash and dry mushrooms. Using a sharp knife, slice each mushroom from the top to the base.

Washing lettuce

All lettuce should be washed before using. Separate leaves, place in sink of ice-cold water, and swish around to loosen dirt and sand. For crispier lettuce, use ice cubes in water. Remove lettuce and place in strainer or salad spinner to drain water.

Tools and Equipment

K itchen tool and equipment lists can be long and complicated. As a household chef, you should collect the proper tools and equipment, such as wire whisks, mixing bowls, baking pans, pots, strainers, potato peelers, etc. The proper tools help make preparation easy and enjoyable. Work in a comfortable area, use a secure cutting board, and clean as you work. This will make cooking much easier.

When preparing seafood dishes, use the right tool for the right job:

Blender/food processor: Use for mixing dressings and making sauces.

Cutting board: Clean and sanitize the cutting board before and after cutting or preparing food products. Do not cut fish and vegetables on the same cutting board without cleaning and sanitizing in between.

Flat spatula: While turning or removing fish from pan, oven, or grill, use a spatula so the fish doesn't fall apart.

Knives: Use a paring knife for cleaning shrimp and a large French knife for cutting vegetables and large pieces of fish. Proper use will keep knife blades sharp. Carefully clean and store knives after each task.

Tongs: Use for turning firm, solid food, such as shrimp and grilled vegetables, on the grill.

Cooking Methods

The methods of cooking seafood are usually grouped into three categories: dry cooking, moist cooking, and a combination of the two.

Dry Cooking Methods

Grilling: Use a heavy metal grate set just above the coals or other heat source, allowing it to heat to the temperature of the grill. Place food directly on the grate and cook well on both sides. When grilling, always watch for flare-ups, as the charred portions of food are carcinogenic.

Oven baking: Cook food in the oven by surrounding it with dry heat. When baking, make sure to monitor the temperature of the oven.

See next page for more about grilling seafood and other delectables.

Moist Cooking Methods

Deep Frying: Deep fry food in hot fat deep enough to completely cover the item being cooked. Use only oils intended for deep frying. Deep frying temperatures should be an average of 300°F to 375°F.

Poaching or steaming: Poaching is cooking food in liquid at or just below the boiling point with just enough liquid to cover the food you are cooking. The temperature depends on what type of food is being prepared. Poaching seafood in water seasoned with lemon juice, dill, thyme, or white wine can add extra flavor.

Steaming retains the food's flavor, shape, and texture better than poaching. Steam food by placing it on a rack or in a special steamer basket over boiling or simmering water in a covered pan.

Combination Cooking Methods

Sauté panfry: To sauté food is to cook it quickly over direct heat in a small amount of oil in a skillet or sauté pan. When sautéing, heat the pan and oil thoroughly before adding ingredients.

More About Grilling

There are hundreds of grills on the market—plain and fancy, charcoal cookers, gas units, electric units, and hibachis. There's one priced right to fit every budget. New grills and cookers that can be used year-round are now available. Propane models are now on the market, as well as electric ones. These grills come with ceramic briquets, pumice, or volcanic rock, which heat very quickly and spread even heat over the entire grill area.

Seafood is fragile. Handle as carefully as possible before and while cooking. An aerosol cooking oil sprayed on the grill before heating will help reduce sticking. Select lean seafood for grilling. Shrimp, dolphin, salmon, and scallops are great for grilling, as are whole, deboned, and cleaned fish. Use only high-quality, fresh seafood when cooking on the grill. Clean and refrigerate it until ready for grilling.

Marinades and barbecue sauces are great ways to bring out extra flavor in grilled seafood. They will tantalize your taste buds. But in regard to flavor, remember that no amount of burning juice or fat is going to add charcoal flavor. When a smoky flavor is desired, scatter hickory, cherry, apple, or hardwood chips (first soaked in water for about a half hour and drained) over briquets just before grilling the seafood.

While grilling, try to avoid flare-ups, which cause unnecessary searing and excess smoke. Flare-ups are frequenty caused by hot fat dripping onto ceramic rocks or briquets. Using a small foil pan centered in the bottom of the grill to catch these drippings can help. If flames are too intense, move food to another section of the grill, rotate the grill, or reduce heat.

Don't ever overcook seafood. Grilling seafood is just like grilling a steak—cook to a medium temperature for best results. Remember, the charred part of any grilled food should not be eaten, as it is a carcinogen.

Grill Recipes: The following recipes call for using a grill (or a broiler, if a grill is not available):

Grilled Tuna with Roasted Pepper Coulis, page 104
Grilled Vegetable Kabobs, page 135
Roasted Corn Salsa, page 42
Roasting and Peeling Peppers, page 131
Seafood Medley with Creamy Tomato-Basil Sauce, page 116
Swordfish Kabobs with Orange-Pecan Barbecue Sauce, page 107

Garnish and Presentation—
The Final Touches

A garnish is an edible and decorative accompaniment to any prepared dish, from appetizer to dessert. Garnishes can be placed around, under, or on food, depending on the dish. Garnishes can be as simple as sprigs of parsley or lemon wedges or as intricate as coulis painting (see page 45). You can use simple ingredients such as lemons, onions, or radishes to add visual appeal to almost any dish. Garnishes should also complement the flavor of the dish, as well as each other.

The presentation of food consists of many factors, from cooking to table design.

Lemon Crowns

Lemons are irreplaceable as a garnish for seafood. The flavor adds zest and the color is pleasing. Lemons are available year-round; when buying, make sure they are bright yellow and firm, but not too hard.

How to cut lemon crowns: Using a paring knife, cut deep zigzags around the lemon as shown. Cut off base of lemon so it will sit up straight.

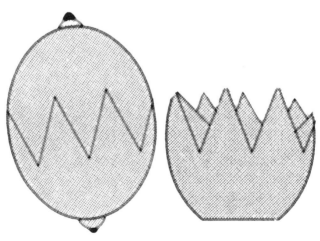

Good presentation is simply the art of noticing how things look. Strive to create order and beauty out of everything you cook. Lay out appetizers, salads, entrées, and desserts in such a way that they highlight the main course. The organization of the plate should establish the main course as the focal point. Some helpful tips on presentation follow:

Color: Great food has great color! Learn to balance the wonderful colors of food in a complementary manner. Try not to cook the color out of your vegetables. Watch the grill marks on fish and avoid serving dark vegetables on a dark plate. Finally, never place a dark plate on a dark tablecloth.

Drinks: Choosing the right wine is easy—try to have both red and white on hand. Also plan on having an assortment of nonalcoholic beverages on hand for your guests. And don't forget to always have plenty of ice!

Table design: Plan table design in advance. Use matching china, correct place settings, proper glassware, and folded napkins. Special centerpieces and candle holders add a nice touch. I always enjoy incorporating a Caribbean theme in the table décor.

Lighting: Lighting should be neither too bright nor too dark. Candles always add a special touch, as can torches placed around the pool.

Music: Music should complement both the mood and the setting. How about a little reggae or Jimmy Buffet? Perhaps some Vivaldi?

RECIPES
Marinades, Sauces, Dressings, Salsas, and Coulis

Marinades

Marinating is allowing food to soak before it is cooked in a mixture of liquid and seasonings blended together to add extra flavor. When making and using marinades, use only glass or stainless-steel bowls, as plastic and wooden containers will absorb the marinade. A blender works best for mixing most marinades.

Marinating in acidic liquids, such as lemon juice, white wine, and vinegars, will help break down muscle fibers as well as add flavor. This is useful for softening tough meats. Oils can be used to add moisture; a good walnut oil or extra-virgin olive oil will also accentuate the flavor. Herbs and spices can enhance marinades. Fresh herbs are superb and should be used exclusively if possible.

Marinades are frequently used to enhance the flavor of seafood before cooking.

Expect marinades to slightly change the color of your entrées. When cooking marinated seafood, watch for possible flare-ups caused by excess oil. Keep in mind that sugar will always cause faster cooking times, so use less heat when marinating with sugar so as not to burn or caramelize it.

To marinate seafood, blend all the ingredients called for in the recipe in a shallow glass or stainless-steel bowl that is just large enough to hold food items when laid out flat. Pour in enough marinade to cover the seafood completely. Next, cover with plastic wrap and let stand in the refrigerator. Seafood should sit in the marinade for at least two hours; longer is recommended for optimum results.

Here are a couple of marinades that I use frequently and really like. After you learn how to prepare and use these marinades, you will want to create your own and experiment with different herbs, seasonings, oils, and acids to make your own favorites.

Classic Herb-Citrus Marinade
¼	cup VEGETABLE OIL
¼	cup WHITE WINE
1	LIME, *squeezed for juice*
1	LEMON, *squeezed for juice*
1	tablespoon GARLIC, *minced*
1	teaspoon THYME, *chopped*
G	teaspoon BLACK PEPPER

Combine all ingredients in a bowl or jar. Refrigerate until ready to use.

Lime & Ginger Oriental Marinade
⅓	cup BURGUNDY WINE
⅓	cup SOY SAUCE
⅓	cup PINEAPPLE JUICE
2	LIMES, *squeezed for juice*
1	tablespoon GARLIC, *minced*
2	tablespoons GINGER, *peeled and minced*

Combine all ingredients in a bowl or jar. Refrigerate until ready to use.

Sauces

E very great seafood cook or chef must learn to prepare great sauces. Whether simple or intricate, a sauce will enhance the flavor and appearance of the food it accompanies. It may also add nutritional value. In this chapter, we will talk about some basic ideas and procedures for making sauces.

Basic Culinary Preparation of Sauces

Basic preparation, as discussed earlier, must also carry over to the art of making sauces. As any great chef will tell you, the true secret to successful cooking is the sauce preparation. A superb Beurre Blanc sauce can quickly turn a fillet of fish into a masterpiece, and there is no limit to what the spicy, tangy Fra Diavolo sauce can accomplish! As you follow the recipes, take the time to prepare the sauces properly. Sauces should be thick enough to coat food lightly, yet still be liquid. The result will complement your seafood, rather than dominate it.

All sauces fall into two categories: warm and cold. You don't have to know all of them. If you learn a few simple procedures for seafood sauce, the rest will come in time. Cold sauces include vinaigrette (oil and vinegar), cocktail, cold mustard, and salsa. Warm sauces include hot butter sauces (butter with seasonings such as herbs, lemon juice, and garlic), béchamel (basic white sauce), mornay (a béchamel with cheese), velouté (a béchamel made with stock instead of cream), egg-based sauces like Hollandaise, and tomato sauces.

Sauces can be thickened with roux, cornstarch, and arrowroot, as well as egg yolks, potato starch, and reduction (see glossary). A roux is a common thickener for savory sauces.

To make a roux, mix equal proportions of fat and flour to make a thick paste. The fat can be butter, margarine, shortening, chicken fat, oil, or rendered meat drippings. Make sure you mix the fat and flour thoroughly to allow the starch granules to swell evenly; otherwise, the roux will not absorb the liquid and your sauce will be thin. In addition, always make sure that you cook out the flour flavor and have no lumps. Roux should be cooked over very low heat for at least 5 minutes, or longer as needed. If a roux is not cooked long enough to displace the raw taste of flour, the unpleasant flavor will dominate even the strongest stocks and seasonings.

Cornstarch is often used when a translucent sauce is desired. When using cornstarch, smoothly blend into it an adequate amount of cold liquid, then add mixture to boiling sauce. Stir constantly to prevent lumping or scorching. If too much cornstarch is added, your sauce will be too thick, so add a little at time until the desired consistency is achieved. Do not overheat cornstarch-based sauces as this will thin them.

The following sauce recipes begin with the cold sauces and move to the hot ones, first the hot butter sauces, then the thickened ones, then the tomato ones. But watch out, I've also thrown in a glaze and a chutney and some other surprises.

Lemon Cocktail Sauce

Cocktail sauce is used as a condiment for hors d'oeuvres and seafood dishes.

½   cup KETCHUP
½   cup CHILI SAUCE, *canned*
1   tablespoon PREPARED HORSERADISH
½   LEMON, *squeezed for juice*
⅛   teaspoon TABASCO SAUCE
¼   teaspoon WORCESTERSHIRE SAUCE

Combine all the ingredients in a mixing bowl. Whisk until well blended. Chill and serve.

Yield: 1+ cups

Red Reef Coral Sauce

An alternative for cocktail sauce that is lighter, yet just as tasty.

¾   cup MAYONNAISE
2   tablespoons KETCHUP
1   tablespoon PREPARED HORSERADISH
2   tablespoons PIMENTO, *chopped fine*

¼   LEMON, *squeezed for juice*

½   *teaspoon* PAPRIKA

⅛   *teaspoon* WORCESTERSHIRE SAUCE

⅛   *teaspoon* TABASCO SAUCE

Combine ingredients in a mixing bowl. Whisk until well blended. Chill and serve.

Yield: 1+ cups

Florida Panther Mustard Sauce

Florida Panther Mustard Sauce is spicy and tangy and is great with stone crabs and crab cakes.

1   *tablespoon* DRY WHITE WINE

⅛   *teaspoon* DRY MUSTARD

½   *cup* MAYONNAISE

¼   *cup* SOUR CREAM

¼   *cup* DIJON MUSTARD

1   *tablespoon* HONEY

¼   LEMON, *squeezed for juice*

In a mixing bowl, combine white wine and dry mustard and blend until dissolved. Add remaining ingredients. Whisk until well blended. Chill and serve.

Yield: 1+ cups

Tartar Sauce with Capers

Homemade tartar sauce tastes a lot better than store-bought sauce.

¾   *cup* MAYONNAISE

2   *tablespoons* SWEET PICKLE RELISH

½   *tablespoon* CAPERS

¼   LEMON, *squeezed for juice*

⅛   *teaspoon* WORCESTERSHIRE SAUCE

2   *drops* TABASCO SAUCE

   SALT *and* PEPPER *to taste*

Combine ingredients in a mixing bowl. Whisk until well blended. Chill and serve.

Yield: 1+ cups

Beurre Blanc

A classic French sauce made with a shallot reduction and whisked cold butter. When seasoned just right, it is excellent with seafood.

2	*tablespoons* SHALLOTS, *minced*
¼	*cup* DRY WHITE WINE
¼	*cup* WHITE WINE VINEGAR
16	*ounces* UNSALTED BUTTER, *cut in 10 pieces*
½	*tablespoon* TARRAGON, *chopped*
½	*tablespoon* CHIVES, *chopped*
½	LEMON, *squeezed for juice*
¼	*teaspoon* WORCESTERSHIRE SAUCE
2	*drops* TABASCO SAUCE
	SALT *and* WHITE PEPPER *to taste*

Place shallots in a heavy saucepan. Then add vinegar and wine. Bring to a simmer over moderate heat. Reduce liquid until almost all liquid has evaporated. Reduce heat and quickly beat in butter, one piece at a time, until all butter is melted. Remove from heat and strain into another pan so the heat will not cause the Beurre Blanc to separate. Add remaining ingredients and adjust flavor with salt and pepper.

Yield: 1+ cups

Papaya Beurre Blanc

¼	*cup* PAPAYA PURÉE *(see page 150)*
2	*tablespoons* SHALLOTS, *minced*
¼	*cup* DRY WHITE WINE
¼	*cup* BALSAMIC VINEGAR
16	*ounces* UNSALTED BUTTER, *cut in 10 pieces*
¼	*tablespoon* TARRAGON, *chopped*
½	*tablespoon* CHIVES, *chopped*
½	LEMON, *squeezed for juice*
¼	*teaspoon* WORCESTERSHIRE SAUCE
2	*drops* TABASCO SAUCE
	SALT *and* WHITE PEPPER *to taste*

When making Papaya Beurre Blanc, follow the recipe for Beurre Blanc but substitute balsamic vinegar for white wine vinegar and add ¼ cup Papaya Purée.

Yield: 1+ cups

Clarified Butter

Clarified butter (also called drawn butter) is great for lobster. Clarified butter has a higher smoking point (since the milk solids have been removed) and may be used to cook at high temperatures.

Using 2 pounds or more of unsalted butter, slowly melt in a small saucepan over low heat. Melt until the milk solids separate (they will sink to the bottom of the pan) and most of the water evaporates. Skim off the top foam. Then, using a big spoon, skim the clear butter off the milky residue in the bottom of the pan. This is clarified butter. Save for later use. It can be stored in the fridge for the same amount of time as regular butter.

Yield: about 3+ cups

Clam Juice and Fish Stock

Stocks are very important ingredients in cooking. A stock is the strained liquid that is the result of cooking meat or fish with vegetables and other seasonings. In the next pages, you will learn some basic stock recipes. In my opinion, fresh stocks are always the best way to go. However, when cooking in a pinch, bottled or canned clam juice purchased in a supermarket will do just fine.

You can use clam juice in making soups, sauces, and in cooking seafood if stock is not available.

Clam Juice

This is simply the liquid in which clams have been cooked. Canned or bottled clam juice may be used instead. Canned clam juice will have the flavor that you will need in making soups, sauces, and in cooking seafood. So I recommend using clam juice if fish stock is not available. You will like the results.

Fish Stock

A good fish stock is made by using fish trimmings from a white fish such as flounder, haddock, turbot, or cod. The fish heads are particularly flavorful. Use salmon only for salmon sauce. Don't cook stock for over 30 minutes and do not stir it while it is cooking!

I   *tablespoon* VEGETABLE OIL
¼   GARLIC CLOVE

1	*pound washed* FISH BONES, HEADS, TAILS, SKINS, *and* TRIMMINGS
5	*cups* WATER
½	*cup* DRY WHITE WINE
1	*teaspoon* SALT
6	BLACK PEPPERCORNS
1	*small bunch fresh* PARSLEY, *with stems*
2	CLOVES
½	BAY LEAF

Mirepoix

¼	ONION, *chopped*
½	CARROT, *chopped*
½	*cup* CELERY, *chopped*

In a large stock pot, combine oil, mirepoix, and garlic; sauté over medium heat until onion is transparent. Stir in fish trimmings. Add water, wine, salt, peppercorns, parsley, cloves, and bay leaf; bring to a boil. Reduce heat and simmer for 30 minutes. Do not stir.

Strain stock through a double-thickness cheesecloth. Discard vegetables, fish, and seasoning. Use stock to make soups, sauces, and gravies. Stock can be frozen for 1 month.

Yield: 3+ cups

Velouté Sauce (Clam or Fish)

One of the "mother sauces," velouté is a stock-based white sauce thickened with a white roux. This sauce is used as a base for making other sauces.

1	*tablespoon* BUTTER
2	*tablespoons* FLOUR
1	*cup* CLAM *or* FISH STOCK (*see page 28*)

Melt butter in a sauté pan and add flour to make a thick paste. Cook for 4 minutes over low heat. Let cool for a few minutes. Add stock to pan gradually, stirring constantly. Reduce and cook for 10 minutes. Stir sauce occasionally. Strain sauce and, if necessary, add more stock to thin it out. The sauce should not be too heavy. Put to the side for later use.

Yield: 1+ cups

Béchamel Sauce

Perhaps the "mother" of all mother sauces.

1	tablespoon	BUTTER
2	tablespoons	FLOUR
1	cup	MILK *or* CREAM

Melt butter in a sauté pan and add flour to make a thick paste. Cook for 4 minutes over low heat. Let cool for a few minutes. Add milk or cream to pan gradually, stirring constantly. Cook and stir for a few minutes. May add more milk or cream to thin it.

Yield: 1+ cups

Mornay Sauce

A béchamel sauce to which cheese has been added, usually Parmesan and Swiss.

¼	cup	PARMESAN CHEESE, *grated*
¼	cup	SWISS CHEESE, *grated*
1+	cups	BÉCHAMEL SAUCE *(see above)*

Make a Béchamel Sauce. Add Parmesan and Swiss cheese and cook over low heat until all cheese is melted, stirring constantly. Add more liquid if needed.

Yield: 1½ cups

Creamy Artichoke Sauce

This sauce can be used for chicken and vegetables just by changing the stock used in the velouté sauce.

⅓	cup	ARTICHOKES HEARTS, *canned*
½	tablespoon	OLIVE OIL
1	teaspoon	GARLIC, *minced*
2	tablespoons	RED WINE VINEGAR
¼	cup	WHITE WINE
¼	cup	HEAVY CREAM
1	cup	CLAM VELOUTÉ SAUCE *(see page 29)*
¼		LEMON, *squeezed for juice*
2	drops	TABASCO SAUCE
		SALT *and* PEPPER *to taste*

Prepare Clam Velouté. Set to the side.

In sauté pan over moderate heat, sauté garlic and artichokes in olive oil. When garlic starts to lightly brown, add vinegar and white wine and reduce by three-quarters. Next, add heavy cream and reduce by half. Add velouté, lemon juice, and Tabasco. Place mixture in blender and purée about 20 seconds, or until sauce is smooth. Place the sauce back in pan and simmer. Add salt and pepper to taste and serve. If too thick, add heavy cream to thin.

Yield: 2 cups

Fra Diavolo Sauce

A devil of a sauce! This sauce is rich, creamy, and has a little bite to it. It will take you some time to prepare, but if you love seafood smothered with a spicy, tangy, red sauce, you'll love this one. First you will prepare a sauce, then prepare the butter into which it is mixed. Pancetta is an Italian bacon that is cured with salt and spices but not smoked.

Fennel Tomato-Basil Sauce

1	tablespoon OLIVE OIL
1	tablespoon GARLIC, *minced*
¼	*cup fresh* FENNEL, *minced (bulb only)*
¼	*cup* WHITE WINE
2	*cups* TOMATO-BASIL SAUCE *(see page 37)*
¼	*teaspoon* TABASCO SAUCE
¼	*teaspoon* RED CRUSHED PEPPER
1	*tablespoon* LOBSTER BASE

Pancetta Bacon Butter

2	*ounces* PANCETTA BACON *or* SMOKED BACON, *ground*
1	*tablespoon* GARLIC, *minced*
8	*ounces* UNSALTED BUTTER
1	*tablespoon* BASIL, *chopped*
1	*tablespoon* LEMON JUICE
¼	*teaspoon* TABASCO SAUCE

Preparing Fennel Tomato-Basil Sauce: Prepare Tomato-Basil Sauce. Combine olive oil, garlic, and fennel in saucepan over moderate heat; sauté for a few minutes until garlic starts to lightly brown. Add white wine and reduce by half. Add Tomato-Basil Sauce, Tabasco, red pepper, and lobster base. Lower heat and simmer for 15 minutes, stirring constantly. Taste and adjust seasoning. Set to the side for later use.

Preparing Pancetta Bacon Butter: Grind pancetta bacon. In sauté pan over moderate heat, combine bacon and garlic; sauté until bacon is cooked. Cool bacon mixture. In mixing bowl, add soft butter, basil, lemon, Tabasco, and bacon mixture; blend thoroughly. Set to the side for later use. Butter mixture can be frozen for use later or will last in refrigerator for days.

Note: The Fennel Tomato-Basil Sauce and the Pancetta Bacon Butter are to be stored separately and are only to be mixed together at time of use. Add the Pancetta Bacon Butter to the Fennel Tomato-Basil Sauce at the last minute for the best results.

Yield: 2 to 3 entrees

Hollandaise Sauce

A delicious and superb sauce for vegetables and poached fish. It's made with butter, egg yolks, and lemon juice and seasoned for extra flavor. Hollandaise is made in a double boiler to prevent egg from scrambling. Keep in mind that too high a heat will break the sauce.

2	EGG YOLKS
1	*tablespoon* WATER
8	*ounces* MELTED BUTTER
1	*tablespoon* LEMON JUICE
2	*drops* TABASCO SAUCE
2	*drops* WORCESTERSHIRE SAUCE
	SALT *and* WHITE PEPPER *to taste*

Place egg yolks and a tablespoon of water into a double boiler over moderate heat. Whip the yolk using a wire whisk until egg starts to fluff. Remove mixing bowl from double boiler if egg starts to cook. Place back in pan and keep whipping until yolks are fluffy and will stand at peaks. Remove from heat and slowly add melted butter, whisking thoroughly until all butter is mixed in. Add remaining ingredients and adjust flavor with salt and pepper. Serve immediately.

Blender Method: In blender, combine egg yolks and lemon juice. Cover and blend for just a moment. At high speed, gradually and steadily add hot butter. Add remaining ingredients and adjust flavor with salt and pepper. Serve immediately.

Yield: 1+ cups

Lime-Ginger Glaze

When making this recipe, use fresh ginger, which is available in most supermarkets.

2 *tablespoons* CORNSTARCH
¼ *cup* CLAM JUICE
1 *tablespoon* CLARIFIED BUTTER
¼ *green* BELL PEPPER, *chopped*
⅛ ONION, *chopped*
¼ *tablespoon* GARLIC, *minced*
1 *teaspoon* GINGER, *chopped*
½ LIME, *cut in half*
¼ ORANGE, *cut in half*
¼ *cup* TERIYAKI SAUCE
¼ *cup* SOY SAUCE
¼ *cup* PINEAPPLE JUICE

Add cornstarch to ¼ cup clam juice and mix into smooth paste; set to the side for later use. In a large saucepan over moderate heat, combine butter, peppers, onion, garlic, and ginger. Cook until vegetables are soft, about 5 to 7 minutes. Add remaining ingredients (except cornstarch mix) and 2 cups of water; simmer for 30 minutes, stirring constantly so sauce does not burn. Reduce sauce by half.

Add cornstarch paste a little at a time, constantly stirring to avoid lumps; sauce will thicken as it cooks. Simmer sauce 5 more minutes, strain, and place to the side for later use.

Yield: about 1½+ cups

Mango Chutney

This spicy condiment contains fruit, vinegar, sugar, and spices. Mangos are in season from May to September. Imported fruit is in the stores sporadically throughout the year. This recipe will take four weeks to make; if you are in a hurry, good mango chutney can be purchased in stores.

1 *ripe* MANGO, *peeled and cut into thin strips*
¾ *cups distilled* WHITE VINEGAR
½ *cup* GRANULATED SUGAR
½ *cup* DARK BROWN SUGAR
1 *cup* ONION, *chopped*
1 GARLIC CLOVE, *minced*

¼ teaspoon BLACK PEPPER
½ teaspoon SALT
½ teaspoon CHILI POWDER
1 tablespoon GINGER ROOT, *chopped*
¾ teaspoon ground CINNAMON
½ teaspoon ground ALLSPICE
½ teaspoon MUSTARD SEED
¼ cup DARK RAISINS
¼ cup DRIED CURRANTS
¾ pound SWEET APPLES, *peeled, cored, and coarsely chopped*

Peel mango and cut into thin strips, discarding seed. Combine mango strips and remaining ingredients in a large mixing bowl. Stir until the mixture is well combined. Cover the bowl and refrigerate overnight.

Bring the mixture to a boil in saucepan over moderately high heat, then reduce heat and simmer. Stir often until the mixture becomes syrupy and thick, about 30 minutes, stirring constantly so chutney does not burn. Transfer the mixture to hot, sterilized jars. Following the instructions that come with jars, seal, cool, and store for at least 4 weeks before using.

Yield: 5 cups

Miami Mango Sauce

Mango is a Miami favorite. Every neighborhood has mango trees in it. Mangos are golden orange and have a fragrant, juicy, sweet, yet tart flesh. When cooking with mangos, the fruit must be carefully carved away from the large seed inside.

1 *medium* MANGO, *ripe*
¼ cup ORANGE JUICE
2 tablespoons DIJON MUSTARD
2 tablespoons DRY WHITE WINE
¼ teaspoon COLEMAN'S DRY MUSTARD
1 tablespoon HONEY
½ cup MANGO CHUTNEY *(see page 33)*

Peel mango and cut into small pieces, discarding seed. Place in small saucepan over moderate heat; add orange juice, Dijon mustard, and honey. In separate bowl, mix white wine and dry mustard until dissolved and pour into mango sauce. Bring to a simmer and reduce in half, stirring constantly. Sauce will thicken while reducing. Place mixture in food processor or blender; add mango chutney and purée for 10 seconds until it makes a smooth sauce; scrape sides of bowl down periodically. Remove from food processor or blender. Place in small bowl and refrigerate until used.

Yield: 2+ cups

Orange-Pecan Barbecue Sauce

Texas has long been famous for its barbecue sauces. Now Florida has its own! This is the perfect sauce for seafood on the grill at your next party. The pecans add a buttery, rich flavor.

2	*strips* BACON
¼	ONION, *chopped*
½	POBLANO PEPPER
¼	RED BELL PEPPER
1	*tablespoon* GARLIC, *minced*
½	*ripe* TOMATO, *no core*
¼	*cup* CIDER VINEGAR
¼	*cup* HONEY
¾	*cup* CHILI SAUCE
1	*cup* TOMATO PASTE
2	*tablespoons* BROWN SUGAR
½	*teaspoon* CHILI POWDER
¼	*cup* ORANGE JUICE, *concentrate*
⅓	*cup* PECANS, *chopped*
	SALT *and* PEPPER *to taste*

In saucepan over moderate heat, combine bacon, onion, Poblano, red pepper, and garlic. Cook until bacon is done and vegetables are tender. Add chopped tomatoes and chili sauce and simmer for 1 minute. Pour mixture into blender or food processor and purée for 10 seconds, stopping two times to scrape the side of the bowl. Place back in pot. Next, add remaining ingredients and whisk thoroughly while sauce simmers. Simmer for 20 minutes, stirring constantly. Set to the side for later use.

Yield: 4+ cups

Orange-Tarragon Sauce

Tarragon is an herb that has narrow, pointed, dark green leaves. Take care when cooking with tarragon—its distinctive flavor can easily dominate other ingredients. In this recipe, you will combine the flavor of tarragon with that of citrus orange to create a wonderful sauce that beautifully accompanies seafood.

- 2 *tablespoons* SHALLOTS, *minced*
- 2 *tablespoons* TARRAGON VINEGAR
- ¼ *cup* DRY WHITE WINE
- ½ *cup* ORANGE JUICE, *concentrated*
- ¼ *cup* HEAVY CREAM
- 1 *cup* CLAM VELOUTÉ (*see page 29*)
- 2 *tablespoons fresh* TARRAGON, *chopped*
  pinch WHITE PEPPER

Make Clam Velouté and set aside.

In a sauté pan over moderate heat, combine shallots, tarragon vinegar, and white wine. Reduce until 2 tablespoons of liquid remain. Next, add orange juice and reduce by half. Add the heavy cream and simmer until reduced by half. Add the velouté, fresh tarragon, and pinch of white pepper for taste; cook over moderate heat for 2 to 3 minutes, stirring constantly. If sauce is too thick, add more cream. If too thin, reduce until sauce reaches the desired consistency.

Yield: 1¾ cups

Roasted Garlic Chili Sauce

In this recipe, you will sweat the peppers until tender, then add garlic and other ingredients. Purée until smooth to make a sauce that goes well with alligator sausage.

- ½ POBLANO PEPPER *or* RED BELL PEPPER, *no seeds or stems*
- ½ GREEN PEPPER, *no seeds or stem*
- ⅛ ONION, *chopped fine*
- 1 *tablespoon* OLIVE OIL
- 2 *tablespoons* RED WINE VINEGAR
- ½ *cup* CHILI SAUCE
- ½ *tablespoon* GRANULATED SUGAR
- ½ LEMON, *squeezed for juice*

1   *clove* ROASTED GARLIC *(see page 131)*
½   *teaspoon* CHILI POWDER
1   *teaspoon* WORCESTERSHIRE SAUCE
½   *teaspoon* TABASCO SAUCE
    SALT *and* PEPPER *to taste*

Make Roasted Garlic and set to the side.

In a saucepan over moderate heat, combine Poblano pepper, green pepper, onion, and olive oil. Sauté for 10 minutes, or until peppers and onion are soft and tender. Add the remaining ingredients (except salt and pepper) and simmer 10 to 12 minutes, stirring constantly.

Place mixture in food processor and purée for 10 seconds, pausing twice to scrape sides of bowl. Adjust flavor with salt and pepper. Remove from blender or food processor and serve warm.

Yield: 2+ cups

Tomato-Basil Sauce

Tomatoes are a member of the nightshade family. While tomatoes have been classified as fruit, most people consider them vegetables.

2   *cups chopped* TOMATO *in juice, canned*
1   *tablespoon* OLIVE OIL
½   *tablespoon* GARLIC, *minced*
¼   *cup* ONION, *finely diced*
1   *tablespoon* PARSLEY, *chopped*
¼   *cup* DRY WHITE WINE
½   *cup* TOMATO PURÉE, *canned*
½   *tablespoons* GRANULATED SUGAR
½   *teaspoon* FENNEL SEED
½   *teaspoon* ANISE SEED
2   *tablespoon* CAPERS, *small*
¼   *cup* BASIL, *chopped*
2   *tablespoons* SALTED BUTTER
    SALT *and* PEPPER *to taste*

Heat olive oil in a saucepan and add garlic, onion, and parsley. Sauté lightly over medium heat for a few minutes, or until garlic and onions start to brown lightly. Do not let garlic and onion burn. Add white wine and reduce in half. Add diced tomatoes and juice, tomato purée, sugar, fennel, anise, and capers over low heat; simmer for 30 minutes (sauce will thicken).

In a blender, purée Tomato-Basil Sauce. Taste and adjust seasoning with salt and pepper. Add chopped basil and butter and stir until butter is melted.

Yield: 3+ cups

Dressings

Dressings in a book about seafood? Sure, every seafood meal needs some fresh vegetables. Here are my favorite dressings for them. And seafoods love dressings too. Check out the lemon-dill one at the end. You'll have a hard time fixing flounder any other way after you've tasted it smothered in this dressing.

Honey Mustard–Poppy Seed Dressing

This classic salad dressing is one that both you and your guests will love. The secret to this recipe is the type of oil used and the blending of the honey and mustard.

¼	cup HONEY, *heated for easier blending*
2	*tablespoons* DIJON MUSTARD
1	*cup* CORN OIL
⅓	*cup* RED WINE VINEGAR
1	*tablespoon* WHITE WINE
1	*teaspoon* POPPY SEEDS
⅛	*teaspoon* SALT

In small mixing bowl, combine hot honey and mustard and blend for 20 seconds. Slowly blend in oil using wire whip; then slowly add vinegar and white wine. Blend for 20 seconds. Add remaining ingredients and blend for 5 seconds. Chill. Whip again before serving.

Yield: 1½+ cups

Florida Citrus-Lemon Dressing

This salad dressing is a treat of fresh citrus and will become a favorite of yours.

3	LEMONS
1	*cup* CORN OIL
1	*tablespoon* GRANULATED SUGAR

⅛   *teaspoon* WHITE PEPPER
⅛   *teaspoon* SALT

Using a zester or grater, grate the outside of three-quarters of a lemon into small mixing bowl. To juice lemon, cut lemon in half on cutting board; with tip of a knife, remove visible seeds. Then, using a citrus reamer or squeezing tightly with hand, squeeze juice from lemon into a small dish; remove any remaining seeds from juice. Add lemon juice and ingredients to zest and blend thoroughly. Taste and adjust flavor if necessary. Chill. Whip again before serving.

Yield: 1+ cups

Balsamic Vinaigrette Dressing

A delicately balanced dressing with fresh vegetables.

¼   *cup* BALSAMIC VINEGAR
½   *cup* CORN OIL
1   *tablespoon* DIJON MUSTARD
⅛   RED BELL PEPPER, *no seeds*
⅛   ONION, *chopped*
1   *small* MUSHROOM, *washed*
1   *tablespoon* PARSLEY, *chopped*
    SALT *and* BLACK PEPPER *to taste*

In blender, combine ingredients and blend thoroughly. Stop two times during blending to scrape down sides of bowl. Chill and serve.

Yield: 1+ cups

Classic Caesar Dressing

This recipe is timeless, and it goes perfectly with Homemade Garlic Croutons (see page 143). It will last only two days in the refrigerator due to the egg yolks used.

1   *tablespoon* GARLIC, *minced*
1   *tablespoon* ANCHOVIES, *chopped*
1   *tablespoon* DIJON MUSTARD
1   *tablespoon* MAYONNAISE
2   EGG YOLKS, *or use pasteurized yolks*
¾   *cup* OLIVE OIL
½   LEMON, *squeezed for juice*

⅛   *teaspoon* WORCESTERSHIRE SAUCE
⅛   *teaspoon* TABASCO SAUCE
2   *tablespoons* PARMESAN CHEESE, *grated*
¼   *teaspoon ground* BLACK PEPPER
2   *tablespoons* RED WINE VINEGAR

Crush garlic and anchovies in small bowl. Add egg yolk, mayonnaise, and Dijon. Mix thoroughly with a wire whisk. Slowly add olive oil until blended. Add lemon juice, Worcestershire, Tabasco, Parmesan, black pepper, and red wine vinegar. Blend thoroughly and serve.

Egg Substitute: Use 4 tablespoons mayonnaise to replace egg yolks.
Yield: 1½ cups

Lemon-Dill Dressing

This dressing is used to smother flounder before baking.

1   *tablespoon all-purpose* FLOUR
1   *tablespoon* GRANULATED SUGAR
½   *teaspoon* COLEMAN'S DRY MUSTARD
½   *cup* MILK
1   *tablespoon* RED WINE VINEGAR
1   *tablespoon* LEMON JUICE
1   *large* EGG YOLK
1   *teaspoon* DILL, *chopped*

In a small saucepan, combine flour, sugar, salt, and mustard; gradually stir in milk to avoid lumping. Cook over moderate heat until mixture begins to boil. Boil for 1 minute, then remove from heat. In mixing bowl, combine vinegar, lemon juice, egg yolk, and dill and mix thoroughly. Add milk mixture a little at a time. Place back into saucepan and simmer over low heat until dressing thickens. Remove dressing from heat and place in mixing bowl.

Yield: 1+ cups

Salsas

Salsa is the Spanish word for "sauce." But it's not a plain old sauce; it's a sauce with that Latin beat. Salsa can be served cooked or raw, made from a variety of vegetables and fruit, but it always has a kick—so that when you taste it, you feel like doing the cha-cha-cha.

Red and Yellow Tomato-Cilantro Salsa

Cilantro is Mexican parsley, and the yellow and red tomatoes will add a nice color to this sauce.

1	*medium ripe* RED TOMATO
1	*medium* YELLOW TOMATO
½	*teaspoon* JALAPEÑO CHILI PEPPER
¼	*medium* RED ONION, *chopped*
2	*tablespoons fresh* CILANTRO, *chopped*
2	*tablespoons* RED WINE VINEGAR
⅛	*teaspoon* GARLIC, *minced*
2	*tablespoons* OLIVE OIL
½	LIME, *squeezed for juice*
4	*drops* TABASCO SAUCE
	SALT *and* PEPPER *to taste*

Prepare a concassé (see page 131) using the two tomatoes. Cut jalapeño pepper in half and remove stem and all seeds. Dice half of the jalapeño. Place tomato concassé and diced jalapeño pepper in mixing bowl. Add onion, cilantro, red wine vinegar, garlic, olive oil, lime juice, and Tabasco; mix thoroughly. Adjust flavor with salt and pepper to taste. Chill for 1 hour to blend the flavors and serve.

Yield: 2+ cups

Roasted Corn Salsa

In this recipe, you will cook corn on the grill for flavor, then cut it off the cob to create a salsa with a tangy, yet sweet, charcoal flavor.

Preheat grill.

2	*large white or yellow* EARS OF CORN
¼	RED PEPPER, *chopped fine*
¼	RED ONION, *chopped fine*
¼	*teaspoon* JALAPEÑO CHILI PEPPER, *diced, no seeds*
1	*tablespoon* CILANTRO, *chopped*
2	*tablespoons* BALSAMIC VINEGAR
¼	*teaspoon* GARLIC, *minced*
2	*tablespoons* CORN OIL
½	LIME, *squeezed for juice*
	SALT *and* PEPPER *to taste*

Shuck corn and cook in pot of boiling water until fully cooked. Rub corn with a little oil to add flavor. Place on preheated grill for 4 to 5 minutes. Do not burn but lightly brown. Using a paring knife, cut kernels off the corn and place in mixing bowl. Add red pepper, onion, jalapeño, cilantro, vinegar, garlic, corn oil, and lime juice; mix thoroughly. Adjust the flavor of the Roasted Corn Salsa with salt and pepper. Place in refrigerator for 2 to 4 hours to chill and for the flavors to blend together.

Yield: 2+ cups

Tropical Fruit Salsa

In this recipe, you will make a unique salsa made of fresh fruit, diced and seasoned. When making this salsa, experiment with some of your favorite fruits.

½	*cup ripe* MANGO, *peeled and diced*
¼	*ripe* PAPAYA, *peeled and diced*
½	*cup* ORANGE, *peeled and diced*
1	KIWI, *peeled and diced*
1	*tablespoon* MINT, *chopped*
2	*tablespoons* OLIVE OIL
2	*tablespoons* RICE VINEGAR
½	LIME, *squeezed for juice*
	SALT *and* PEPPER *to taste*

Cut the mango and papaya in half lengthwise and, using a large spoon, scoop out seeds; discard. Peel mango, papaya, orange (remove the seeds), and kiwi. Dice fruit in quarter-inch cubes and place in large mixing bowl. Add mint, olive oil, vinegar, and lime; gently mix thoroughly. Adjust flavor of the salsa with salt and pepper to taste. Chill for 1 hour to blend the flavors.

Fruit Substitutes: Strawberries, pineapple, peaches, pears, berries, grapefruits, and more.

Yield: 2+ cups

Sunset Coulis Collection

Coulis are used to paint entrées for a special effect. This is truly food art at its finest. In this collection, I offer several examples that will add color and taste to almost any dish and blend well with the Florida cuisine of today and of years to come.

The Sunset Coulis Collection consists of five simple sauces that have color and are easy to make:

Hibiscus Coulis
Mango-Wasabi Coulis
Cilantro Pesto Coulis
Sun-Dried Tomato Coulis
Roasted Red and Yellow Pepper Coulis

Use coulis to paint entrées for a dazzling presentation. Once coulis are prepared, they will be placed in squeeze bottles. When ready to serve dishes, pick up squeeze bottle and paint the top of plate and food.

Art Studio Coulis Painting Ideas

The plate is the canvas, the sauces are the paint, and the ladles and squeeze bottles are the brushes. Use your imagination! Sauce painting uses contrast and composition, similar to canvas painting. One of my favorite ways is to use a squeeze bottle to paint designs using the liquid sauce. The coulis must be smooth and liquid enough to flow easily through the bottle. On this and the following page are some diagrams of my favorite patterns.

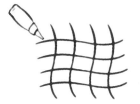

Recipes

Hibiscus Coulis

This coulis is made with fresh ginger and beets and is a deep red color.

1	teaspoon fresh GINGER, *peeled and chopped*
¼	*cup* DRY WHITE WINE
½	*cup* BEETS *with juice*
2	*tablespoons* MAYONNAISE
	SALT *and* WHITE PEPPER *to taste*

Combine chopped ginger, white wine, and beet juice in a small saucepan and simmer until liquid is reduced in half. Remove from heat and place all ingredients in food processor; purée for 1 to 2 minutes, stopping twice to scrape down sides of bowl. Strain the coulis by placing it in a fine strainer and pressing it (remember to place a bowl under the strainer). Save the liquid and discard pulp. Place sauce in squeeze bottle—coulis is now ready for painting. If necessary, cut a small bit off tip of squeeze bottle to allow coulis to pass through.

Yield: 1 cup

Mango-Wasabi Coulis

Wasabi is a Japanese horseradish available as a paste or a powder that is blended with liquid. The combination of mango and wasabi puréed together is a treat.

½	*cup ripe* MANGO *or* MANGO PURÉE
2	*tablespoons* MAYONNAISE
½	*teaspoon* CURRY POWDER
1	*teaspoon* DRY WHITE WINE
1	*teaspoon* WASABI
	SALT *and* WHITE PEPPER *to taste*

Peel mango and remove seeds. Place mango, mayonnaise, curry powder, white wine, and wasabi in a food processor. Purée for 1 to 2 minutes, stopping twice to scrape down sides of bowl. Sauce must be well puréed. Adjust flavor with salt and pepper. Strain the coulis by placing it in a fine strainer and pressing it (remember to place a bowl under the strainer). Save the liquid and discard pulp. Place sauce in squeeze bottle—coulis is now ready for painting. If necessary, cut a small bit off tip of squeeze bottle to allow coulis to pass through.

Yield: 2 cups

Cilantro Pesto Coulis

Pesto is an uncooked sauce made with fresh basil, garlic, pine nuts, Parmesan cheese, and olive oil. In this recipe, you will substitute cilantro for basil, as cilantro has a flavor that fits well with highly seasoned food.

¼	*cup* PINE NUTS	
1	*cup* OLIVE OIL	
2	*tablespoons* PARMESAN CHEESE, *grated*	
¼	*cup* CILANTRO, *chopped*	
1	*tablespoon* GARLIC, *minced*	
	SALT *and* WHITE PEPPER *to taste*	

Place all ingredients in blender or food processor and blend thoroughly, pausing five to six times to scrape mixture down. Adjust flavor with salt and white pepper. Strain the coulis by placing it in a fine strainer and pressing it (remember to place a bowl under the strainer). Save the liquid and discard pulp. Place sauce in squeeze bottle—coulis is now ready for painting. If necessary, cut a small bit off tip of squeeze bottle to allow coulis to pass through.

Yield: 1 cup

Sun-Dried Tomato Coulis

A California favorite that is tasty, yet simple and easy to make.

½	*cup* TOMATO SAUCE (*you can use the* TOMATO-BASIL SAUCE *on page 37 if you wish*)	
¼	*cup* SUN-DRIED TOMATOES	
2	*tablespoons* MAYONNAISE	
1	*teaspoon* DRY WHITE WINE	

If using sun-dried tomatoes, soak in boiling water for 30 minutes to soften, or follow the directions on package. Place all ingredients in blender or food processor and blend thoroughly, pausing three to four times to scrape mixture down until smooth. Adjust flavor with salt and white pepper. If coulis is thick, add a drop of white wine to thin. Strain the coulis by placing it in a fine strainer and pressing it (remember to place a bowl under the strainer). Save the liquid and discard pulp. Place sauce in squeeze bottle—coulis is now ready for painting. If necessary, cut a small bit off tip of squeeze bottle to allow coulis to pass through.

Yield: 1 cup

Roasted Red and Yellow Pepper Coulis

In this recipe, you will use red and yellow bell peppers to make a sweet pepper sauce.

Preheat grill.

1	*each*, ROASTED RED *and* YELLOW BELL PEPPER
1	*tablespoon* SHALLOTS, *minced*
2	*tablespoons* RED WINE VINEGAR
¼	*cup* DRY WHITE WINE
¼	*cup* HEAVY CREAM
1	*cup* CLAM VELOUTÉ (*see page 29*)
1	*tablespoon* CHIVES, *chopped*
	SALT *and* PEPPER *to taste*

Place peppers on hot grill and cook on all sides until the skins start to turn black and shrivel up (a broiler can be used instead of the grill). Remove from grill and place in a bowl; seal top with plastic wrap. After about 10 minutes the skins will start to peel. Remove peppers from bowl and rinse under running water to peel off skins. Remove seeds and stems from the inside. Set to the side.

> Sweet pepper is a member of the bell pepper family.

In sauté pan over moderate heat, combine shallots, vinegar, and white wine. Reduce until 1 tablespoon of liquid is left. Add heavy cream and reduce in half. Add velouté and chives. Simmer 1 minute.

In blender, place half of reduced sauce and roasted red pepper; purée 10 seconds. Place in small pan to keep warm. Wash blender and repeat with yellow pepper, using the remaining reduced sauce. Keep colors separate. Set aside in a warm place for later use. If sauces are thin, reduce in saucepan over moderate heat until thickened.

Yield: 2 cups

Recipes
Seafood

Appetizers

Clams on the Half Shell

Clams on the half shell are a treat! Serve with crackers and hot sauce.

Many of the following appetizers call for lemon crowns as a garnish. See page 50 for instructions on cutting lemon crowns.

12 SHELL CLAMS (*littlenecks or cherrystones*)
1 *cup* LEMON COCKTAIL SAUCE (*see page 25*)
6 LEMON WEDGES

Shuck clams (see page 89). Arrange on a bed of crushed ice in six shallow bowls or plates. Place six half-shell calms on the ice with a small container of Lemon Cocktail Sauce in the center. Garnish with lemon wedges.

Yield: 2 servings

Steamed Clams with White Wine and Garlic Sauce

The sweet flavor of white wine and the tang of garlic will add a spicy zest to your clams in a classic, yet tantalizing display.

24   LITTLENECK CLAMS, *fresh, washed, and cleaned*
 2   *ounces* BUTTER
 1   *tablespoon* GARLIC, *minced*
 ½   *cup* DRY WHITE WINE
 ½   *cup* WATER
 ½   LEMON, *squeezed for juice*
 2   *tablespoons fresh* PARSLEY, *chopped*

Garnish
    LEMON WEDGES, PARSLEY SPRIGS

Wash clams in water and set to the side. Melt butter in a deep saucepan over moderate heat. Add garlic; cook until it becomes transparent. Add clams, white wine, water, lemon juice, and chopped parsley to the garlic butter. Cover and simmer 6 to 9 minutes until clams have all opened. Do not overcook clams, as they will become tough and chewy.

To serve, divide clams between two large soup bowls. Pour excess juice over top. To garnish, place lemon wedges and parsley sprigs to the side of bowls. Sprinkle with extra chopped parsley.

Yield: 2 servings

Bahama Conch-Papaya Pancakes with Chili Sour Cream

A unique dish that is easy to prepare. By adding the sweet flavor of papaya and conch, you have a real Floridian treat. This is accompanied by Chili Sour Cream, with which you can paint the plate.

Conch-Papaya Pancakes
 2   *ounces* CONCH MEAT, *ground or food processed (if using food processor, freeze meat for 15 minutes prior to preparation)*
 ¼   *cup* PAPAYA, *finely diced*
 ½   *cup all-purpose* FLOUR
 1   *tablespoon* GRANULATED SUGAR
 1   *medium* EGG, *separated*
 ¾   *cup* MILK
 1   *tablespoon* MELTED BUTTER
 ½   *tablespoon* CHIVES, *chopped*
 ½   *teaspoon* OLD BAY SEASONING
    OIL *for sautéing*

Conch Shells are spiral-shaped; when you hold one up to your ear, you can hear the roar of the ocean.

Chili Sour Cream
¼ *cup* SOUR CREAM
1 *tablespoon* LIME JUICE
¾ *tablespoon* CHILI POWDER

Lemon Cocktail Sauce (see page 25)

Garnish
LEMON CROWNS, PARSLEY SPRIGS

Place ground conch in strainer and squeeze out excess juice. Peel papaya and remove seeds. Dice papaya into small pieces. In a mixing bowl, sift in flour and sugar. Next, add egg yolk, milk, and melted butter and, using a whisk, whip until smooth. Add conch, papaya, chives, and Old Bay Seasoning. Mix thoroughly and refrigerate for 1 hour. Beat egg white to soft peaks in small mixing bowl. Fold into chilled conch batter.

Heat oil in sauté pan over moderate heat. Carefully pour pancake batter into pan, forming four medium-size pancakes. Sauté on each side until light golden brown. Remove from pan and place on two plates. Serve with Chili Sour Cream and Lemon Cocktail Sauce. Garnish plates with lemon crowns and parsley sprigs.

To prepare Chili Sour Cream, combine sour cream, lime juice, and chili powder in a small mixing bowl. Whip thoroughly and serve with pancakes.

Yield: 2 servings

Key West Stone Crab with Florida Panther Mustard Sauce

Served cold with this tangy mustard sauce, the stone crabs will just melt in your mouth!

6 *large* STONE CRAB CLAWS, *cooked*
¼ *head* LEAF LETTUCE, *washed*

Sauces
FLORIDA PANTHER MUSTARD SAUCE *(see page 26)*
LEMON COCKTAIL SAUCE *(see page 25)*

Garnish
LEMON CROWNS
KALE

Using handle of lobster crackers, crack stone crab claws on each joint and claw. Be careful not to shatter shell completely. Place three claws on each plate covered with leaf lettuce. Serve with Florida Panther Mustard Sauce and Lemon Cocktail Sauce. Garnish with lemon crowns and kale and serve ice cold.

Florida stone crabs are available from October through April.

Yield: 2 servings

Herb-Crabmeat Cheese Dip with Toasted Pita Triangles

A simple appetizer that will tantalize your taste buds. Pita triangles, when toasted, are great for dipping. The dip is scrumptious!

Preheat oven to 350°F.

Herb-Crabmeat Cheese Dip

4	ounces CRABMEAT
1	tablespoon BUTTER
1	teaspoon GARLIC, *minced*
¼	cup WHITE WINE
¼	cup HEAVY CREAM
¼	LEMON, *squeezed for juice*
1	cup CLAM VELOUTÉ (*see page 30*)
4	ounces CHEDDAR CHEESE, *shredded*
1	tablespoon CHIVES, *chopped*
⅛	teaspoon TABASCO SAUCE
⅛	teaspoon WORCESTERSHIRE SAUCE
	SALT *and* PEPPER *to taste*

Pita Bread Triangles

4	large PITA ROUNDS, *cut in eighths to form triangles*
¼	cup BUTTER, *melted*
	GRANULATED GARLIC, *as needed*
	PAPRIKA, *as needed*

Garnish

LEMON CROWNS, PARSLEY SPRIGS

To make dip, check over crabmeat for pieces of shell. Using sauté pan, melt butter over moderate heat; add garlic and sauté till light brown. Add white wine and continue cooking for 2 to 3 minutes. Add heavy cream and lemon juice and simmer until it reduces in half. Stir in velouté. Add cheddar cheese and stir until smooth. Add crabmeat, chives, Tabasco, and Worcestershire. Mix thoroughly. Add salt and pepper to taste.

To make pita bread triangles, take pita rounds and cut in eighths to form triangles. Lay out pita triangles on baking pan and lightly coat with melted butter. Sprinkle with granulated garlic and paprika. Bake pita triangles in oven at 350°F for 4 minutes or until pita starts to toast. Remove from oven; serve warm.

Place Herb-Crabmeat Cheese Dip in medium-size bowl and put in middle of large platter. Surround with pita triangles and serve. Garnish plates with lemon crowns and parsley sprigs.

Yield: 2 servings

Sarasota Deviled Crab

So devilishy good that you will find yourself making these deviled crabs all the time.

Preheat oven to 350°F.

½	pound CRABMEAT
1	tablespoon ONION, *chopped*
1½	tablespoons BUTTER, *melted*
1	tablespoon all-*purpose* FLOUR
6	tablespoons MILK
¼	teaspoon SALT
	small *dash* WHITE PEPPER
¼	teaspoon POWDERED MUSTARD
¼	teaspoon WORCESTERSHIRE
¼	teaspoon SAGE
	small *dash* CAYENNE PEPPER
½	tablespoon LEMON JUICE
½	EGG, *beaten*
½	tablespoon PARSLEY, *chopped*
2	tablespoons *dry* BREAD CRUMBS

Garnish

LEMON WEDGES, PARSLEY SPRIGS

Remove any shell or cartilage from crabmeat. Sauté onion in butter until tender. Blend in flour. Add milk gradually and cook until thick, stirring constantly. Add seasonings and lemon juice. Stir a little of the hot sauce into egg; add the remaining sauce, stirring constantly. Add parsley and crabmeat. Place in two well-greased, individual baking shells or 7-ounce custard cups. Combine butter and bread crumbs; sprinkle over top of each shell. Bake at 350°F for 15 to 20 minutes or until middle of deviled crab and egg mixture has set up and cooked. Garnish with parsley and lemon wedges.

Yield: 2 servings

Crabmeat Florentine Mushroom Caps with Mornay Sauce

Mushrooms are one of nature's most versatile foods. In this recipe, we will stuff mushroom caps with crabmeat and place them on top of a bed of seasoned spinach.

Preheat oven to 325°F.

8	*large* MUSHROOMS
3	*ounces fresh leaf* SPINACH, *washed and no stems*
¼	*cup* DRY WHITE WINE

Crabmeat Stuffing

3	*ounces* BUTTER
¼	*cup* ONION, *chopped fine*
¼	*tablespoon* GARLIC, *minced*
¼	*cup* RED BELL PEPPER, *chopped fine*
4	*ounces* CRABMEAT *(check for shells)*
¼	*cup* HEAVY CREAM
¼	*cup* PARMESAN CHEESE, *grated*
¾	*cup white* BREAD CRUMBS, *fresh*
I	*tablespoon* LEMON JUICE

Mornay Sauce (see page 30)

Garnish

LEMON CROWNS, PARSLEY SPRIGS

For stuffing, melt butter in sauté pan over moderate heat. Add onion, garlic, and red pepper. Sauté until onion is translucent and pepper is soft. Next, add crabmeat and heavy cream and cook for 2 to 3 minutes, stirring constantly. Remove from heat and place in mixing bowl; add Parmesan cheese, bread crumbs, and lemon juice. Mix thoroughly and set to the side.

Pull out stems of mushroom caps and wash mushrooms. Place mushroom caps in a pot of boiling water and let sit 4 minutes. Remove caps from water and place in a baking pan. Heap large portions of stuffing mix in mushroom caps. Bake in oven at 325°F for 8 to 10 minutes or until done.

In a separate sauté pan over moderate heat, poach spinach in white wine and water for 2 to 3 minutes. Remove and drain off excess water. Unfold leaves and lay out on two plates. Place stuffed mushroom caps on top and dribble with Mornay Sauce. If needed, place plate in oven for a few minutes to heat spinach before serving; be careful when removing hot plate from oven. Garnish with lemon crowns and parsley sprigs.

Yield: 2 servings

Roasted Poblano Peppers with Crabmeat–Cream Cheese Stuffing

Florida produces an abundance of fresh bell peppers year-round. In this recipe, you will take roasted peppers and stuff them with crabmeat and cream cheese, then bread with cornmeal.

2	*large roasted* POBLANO PEPPERS
⅓	*cup all-purpose* FLOUR
1	EGG *(for egg wash)*
½	*cup* CORNMEAL
2	*cups* KALE, *shredded*
	OIL *for sautéing*

Crabmeat–Cream Cheese Stuffing

3	*ounces* CRABMEAT, *checked for shells*
4	*ounces* CREAM CHEESE, *room temperature*
½	*teaspoon* CHILI POWDER
2	*tablespoons* CHIVES, *chopped*

Roasted Corn Salsa (see page 42)

Garnish

HIBISCUS COULIS *(see page 47)*
LEMON WEDGES, PARSLEY SPRIGS

To make stuffing, add crabmeat, cream cheese, chili powder, and chives to a mixing bowl. Mix thoroughly and set to the side.

To prepare the Poblano peppers, follow the recipe for roasting and peeling peppers on page 131. Make an incision cut on one side of each pepper and remove all the seeds. Open pepper and gently fill with crab-meat stuffing.

Using breading procedures on page 94, dip peppers in flour, egg wash, and cornmeal, coating all sides. Use toothpicks to hold together, if necessary.

In a sauté pan, add oil and fry breaded peppers over moderate heat. Cook until golden brown and crispy on all sides. Remove peppers and place on paper to drain grease. Using two plates, place shredded kale on one side of plate and pile up high. Next place cooked stuffed pepper on kale so stem is on kale and other end is on clear part of plate. Dribble Roasted Corn Salsa around clear end of plate. Garnish with lemon wedges and parsley sprigs.

Painting with Hibiscus Coulis from Sunset Coulis Collection: Following recipe, prepare coulis ahead of time and place in squeeze bottle, allowing it to cool to room temperature prior to use. When ready to serve seafood, use Hibiscus Coulis and painting techniques on page 46 to create designs on top of seafood and plate. Always paint the plates right before serving seafood.

Yield: 2 servings

Key Largo Shrimp with Garlic-Parmesan Butter

When making this dish, use jumbo or extra-large shrimp, which will be smothered with a tantalizing Garlic-Parmesan Butter Sauce that will melt in your mouth!

Preheat oven to 350°F.

8	*large or jumbo* SHRIMP, *peeled and deveined*
	PAPRIKA *to taste*

This recipe is a favorite at the Firehouse Restaurant in Boca Raton.

Garlic-Parmesan Butter

6	*ounces* UNSALTED BUTTER
¼	*tablespoon* GARLIC, *minced*
2	*tablespoons* WHITE WINE
½	*cup* PARMESAN CHEESE, *grated*
⅛	*teaspoon* GRANULATED GARLIC
¼	*tablespoon* WORCESTERSHIRE SAUCE
2	*tablespoons* PARSLEY, *chopped*

¼   LEMON, *squeezed for juice*

Yellow Saffron Rice (see page 140)

Garnish

LEMON CROWNS, PARSLEY SPRIGS

Melt unsalted butter in sauté pan over moderate heat. Remove from heat and add remaining ingredients listed for the butter. Blend thoroughly. Set to the side.

Peel and devein shrimp. Butterfly shrimp using a paring knife (see page 119). Be sure to cut almost all the way through when butterflying. Lay shrimp flat in a pie pan, red side down.

Thoroughly whip Garlic-Parmesan Butter and distribute evenly over shrimp. Sprinkle paprika on top. Bake at 350°F for 7 to 8 minutes or until done. Remove from oven and place on two plates with Yellow Saffron Rice. Pour excess sauce over shrimp. Garnish with lemon crowns and parsley sprigs.

Yield: 2 servings.

South Beach Shrimp Wings with Garlic-Raspberry Sauce

A great appetizer. Medium-size shrimp are lightly coated and fried, then topped with Garlic-Raspberry Sauce.

Preheat deep fryer to 350°F.

1   *pound medium* SHRIMP, *peeled and deveined*
1   *cup* BUTTERMILK
¾   *cup all-purpose* FLOUR
   OIL *for deep frying*

Garlic-Raspberry Sauce
¼   *cup* CLAM JUICE
2   *tablespoons* CORNSTARCH
1   *teaspoon* OLIVE OIL
1   *tablespoon* GARLIC, *minced*
¼   *cup* GREEN BELL PEPPER, *chopped*
¼   *cup* ONION, *chopped*
¼   *cup* SHERRY
¼   *cup* RASPBERRY VINEGAR
¼   *cup* RASPBERRIES, *fresh*

½   *cup* LIGHT CORN SYRUP

3   *tablespoons* KETCHUP

2   *tablespoons* SOY SAUCE

⅛   *teaspoon* POWDERED GINGER

      SALT *and* PEPPER *to taste*

Garnish

      LEMON CROWNS

2   SCALLION FLOWERS *(see page 130)*

To make sauce, place ½ cup of the cold clam juice in a bowl and mix in the cornstarch to make a paste. In a saucepan over moderate heat, combine oil, garlic, green pepper, and onion and sauté until garlic starts to lightly brown. Now add sherry and reduce 1 minute. Then add vinegar, raspberries, corn syrup, ketchup, soy sauce, and ginger powder and bring to a boil, stirring constantly. Place in a blender and purée, stopping three times to push contents down into blender. Put back in saucepan, add mixture of cornstarch and clam juice, and simmer until thickened. Flavor with salt and pepper. Set to the side.

Place peeled and deveined shrimp in a bowl of buttermilk for 1 hour. Remove from bowl and thoroughly coat in flour. Deep fry shrimp at 350°F for 2 to 3 minutes until brown. Toss shrimp and sauce in bowl, then divide between two plates and serve. Put excess sauce in gravy boat and serve with shrimp. Garnish with lemon crowns and scallion flowers.

Yield: 2 servings

"Caribbean" Baked Oysters with Tomatillo Salsa and Jicama

The unique blend of tomatillo salsa and the nutty flavor of jicama, combined with the unique flavor of cilantro and smothered over oysters, is a visual delight. And wait till you experience the flavor!

> Tomatillo: A green, tomato-like vegetable from Mexico.

Preheat oven to 350°F.

12   *medium to large fresh* OYSTERS, *shucked in half*

1   *cup coarse* SEA SALT

Tomatillo Salsa

4   TOMATILLOS, *peeled and rough chopped (see Concassé, page 131)*

¼   *cup* RED ONION, *chopped fine*

2   *tablespoons* OLIVE OIL

1   *tablespoon* RED WINE VINEGAR

1   *tablespoon* CILANTRO, *chopped*
½   *teaspoon* GARLIC, *minced*
¼   LEMON, *squeezed for juice*
     SALT *and* PEPPER *to taste*

Jicama

2   *large* JICAMA, *peeled, sliced thin, and julienned*
1   *tablespoon* OLIVE OIL *for sautéing*
¼   *teaspoon* GARLIC, *minced*
¼   *cup* DRY WHITE WINE
½   LEMON, *squeezed for juice*
     SALT *and* PEPPER *to taste*

Garnish

LEMON CROWNS, PARSLEY SPRIGS

Commercial, mechanical oyster shuckers are by far the easiest way to extract the oyster from its shell. However, shucking by hand is quite common and convenient, as commercial shuckers are not very common. Prior to shucking oysters, wash and rinse them thoroughly in cold water. Place one on a table, flat shell up, and hold it in one hand while forcing an oyster knife into the opening at or near the thin end with the other. For easier knife insertion, the thin end, or "bill," may be broken off with a hammer. Once opened, cut the large adductor muscle close to the flat upper shell and remove shell. Cut the lower end of the same muscle, which is attached to the deep half of the shell. After shucking, be sure to examine the oysters for small pieces of shell that may have adhered to the muscle.

Preparing Tomatillo Salsa (salsa may be prepared the day before): Following recipe for Tomato Concassé on page 131, peel and coarsely chop tomatillos. In mixing bowl, combine all ingredients for tomatillo sauce. Mix thoroughly.

Preparing jicama: Heat olive oil over moderate heat in sauté pan. Add jicama and garlic. Sauté for 1 to 2 minutes, then add white wine and lemon juice. Simmer until jicama is soft, yet not overcooked. Add salt and pepper to taste.

Lay shucked oysters out on baking pan. On top of oysters, place a heaping spoonful of Tomatillo Salsa. Bake oysters in oven for 5 to 8 minutes at 350°F until inside of oyster is cooked.

Remove oysters from oven and place on plate covered with coarse sea salt. Place sautéed jicama on top of each oyster. Garnish with lemon crowns and parsley sprigs.

Yield: 2 servings

Baked Dolphin Fingers with Miami Mango Sauce

Dolphin is a native fish and oh, so sweet when fresh! Especially when served with a light mustard sauce that is mango sweet, yet with a slight bite to it.

Preheat oven to 350°F.

12	ounces	DOLPHIN FILLET, *skinless and deveined*
2	tablespoons	MELTED BUTTER
¼	cup	DRY WHITE WINE
1		LEMON, *squeezed for juice*

Miami Mango Sauce (see page 34)

Garnish

1   MANGO, *sliced*
     LEMON CROWNS, PARSLEY SPRIGS

Prepare Miami Mango Sauce and place to the side in a warm spot.

Cut dolphin fillets in long strips, approximately 2 ounces per portion. Each should be about finger size.

In a baking pan coated with butter, lay out dolphin fingers. Add white wine, lemon juice, and water. Spread half of Miami Mango Sauce on fish and bake at 350°F for 6 to 8 minutes or until done.

On two plates, place dolphin fingers in fan style, yet leave room at short end of fan for lemon crown. Dribble with the extra Miami Mango Sauce.

For garnish, see diagram below. Peel and deseed mango; cut into 2-inch wedges. Using a paring knife, make long cuts lengthwise in mango wedges. Make cuts almost to the top and all the way through the mango wedges. Using your hand, gently press mango down into a fan-shaped garnish. Place on each side of lemon crown. Garnish with parsley sprigs.

Yield: 2 servings

Lobster-Stuffed Eggs

Mom made stuffed eggs, but wait until she tastes yours!

½   pound cooked LOBSTER MEAT *(see page 78)*
½   teaspoon ONION, *grated*
½   teaspoon GREEN PEPPER, *chopped fine*
1   teaspoon PIMENTO, *chopped fine*
½   tablespoon CHILI SAUCE
⅓   cup MAYONNAISE *or* SALAD DRESSING
9   hard-cooked EGGS
     PARSLEY

To hard-cook eggs, place 9 eggs in a single layer in a saucepan. Add enough water to cover eggs by at least 1 inch. Cover and bring water to a boil over high heat. Turn off heat. Remove pan from burner to prevent further boiling. Let stand covered for 15 to 17 minutes. Drain, then run cold water over eggs or place in ice water until completely cooled. Peel eggs by tapping all around the shell with a knife to crack all over. Peel shell away under cold running water.

This is a great appetizer to serve at a cocktail party.

Chop lobster meat. Add onion, green pepper, pimento, chili sauce, and mayonnaise mix. Chill. Cut eggs in half lengthwise and remove yolks. Place lobster mixture in egg whites. Garnish with parsley.

Yield: 18 stuffed egg halves

Lobster Chutney Triangles with Tropical Fruit Salsa

This is my version of large ravioli, but stuffed with the sweetness of lobster and chutney! The triangles will be cooked in water, then sautéed in olive oil, garlic, and fresh basil. The sautéing makes this a special treat.

Lobster Chutney Mix

3   ounces cooked LOBSTER MEAT
½   cup MANGO CHUTNEY *(see page 34)*
1   teaspoon DIJON MUSTARD
½   LIME, *squeezed for juice*
2   tablespoons OLIVE OIL
½   tablespoon GARLIC, *minced*
2   tablespoons fresh BASIL, *chopped*
     pinch of BLACK PEPPER

Pasta Dough (see page 146)
    FLOUR *as needed*
    EGG WASH *as needed*

Tropical Fruit Salsa (see page 43)

Garnish
  ¼ *cup* MANGO-WASABI COULIS *(see page 47)*
    LEMON CROWNS, PARSLEY SPRIGS

Making Lobster Chutney Mix: Cook lobster meat in boiling water for 4 to 5 minutes or until done. Chop lobster meat into small pieces. In a mixing bowl, thoroughly mix all ingredients listed for lobster chutney.

Preparing pasta triangles: On a cutting board dusted with flour, roll out pasta dough into a thin sheet and cut into four 4 x 4–inch squares. Place equal amounts of lobster chutney mix on each square. Fold corner to opposite corner to form triangle. Brush egg wash on inside of pasta where fold comes together; this will help seal triangles. Pinch edges together with the end of a fork to seal tightly.

Bring large saucepan of water to a boil and cook each triangle for 3 to 5 minutes. Remove from water and pat dry. In sauté pan over moderate heat, combine olive oil, garlic, basil, and black pepper. When oil is hot, sauté triangles on each side until they start to lightly brown. Remove triangles and place on serving plates. Serve with Tropical Fruit Salsa. Garnish with lemon crowns and parsley sprigs.

Painting with Mango-Wasabi Coulis: Prepare coulis ahead of time and place in squeeze bottle. When ready to serve seafood, use Mango-Wasabi Coulis and painting techniques on page 46 to create designs on top of seafood and plate. Always paint the plates immediately before serving.

Yield: 2 servings

Baked Escargot with Brie Butter

Brie cheese complements the flavor of escargot, a favorite of mine.

Preheat oven to 325°F.

  10 *large* SNAILS, *canned*
   1 *tablespoon* BUTTER

¼   *teaspoon* GARLIC, *minced*

2   *tablespoons* PERNOD LIQUEUR

Brie Butter

2   *2.2-ounce individual* BRIE CHEESES

1   *tablespoon* BUTTER

1   *teaspoon* BRANDY

1   *teaspoon all-purpose* FLOUR

½   *tablespoon* CHIVES, *chopped*

Garnish

LEMON CROWNS, PARSLEY SPRIGS

Wash snails. Melt 1 tablespoon butter in sauté pan over moderate heat. Add snails, garlic, and Pernod; sauté for 2 minutes, stirring constantly. Remove from heat and place to the side.

To make Brie Butter, put ingredients for Brie Butter in food processor and blend, pausing three or four times to scrape down sides of bowl. Remove Brie Butter from food processor and place in small bowl. Refrigerate until ready to use.

In two escargot dishes or two small 3 x 3–inch baking dishes, arrange escargot, then heap ample portions of Brie Butter over top of snails. Bake in oven at 325°F for 7 to 9 minutes or until done. Remove from oven and place on large plate with doilies. Garnish plate with lemon crowns and parsley sprigs.

Yield: 2 servings

Soups and Salads

Everglades Alligator and Sausage Gumbo

In this recipe we will use alligator, sausage, and gumbo filé to create a stewlike soup that will have an incomparable flavor!

¼   *pound* ALLIGATOR MEAT, *ground*

1   *slice raw* BACON

¼   *pound* MEDIUM-HOT ITALIAN SAUSAGE, *cut in bite-size pieces*

½   *tablespoon* GARLIC, *minced*

2   *tablespoons* PARSLEY, *chopped*

½   *cup* ONION, *chopped*

½   *cup* RED BELL PEPPER, *chopped*

½   *cup* GREEN BELL PEPPER, *chopped*

½   *cup* OKRA, *sliced*

1   *quart* FISH STOCK *or* CLAM JUICE *(see page 28)*

1   *tablespoon* LONG-GRAIN WHITE RICE

1   *cup chopped* TOMATOES *in juice, canned*

1   BAY LEAF

1   *tablespoon* GUMBO FILÉ *(available in most food stores)*

   SALT *and* PEPPER *to taste*

   HOT SAUCE *to taste*

> The word "gumbo" is a derivation of the African word for okra.

Before you start making this soup, make stock and set to the side.

Grind alligator meat and bacon together. If using a food processor, freeze meat for 15 minutes prior to grinding.

In a saucepan over moderate heat, sauté alligator meat, bacon, sausage, garlic, and parsley. Cook until garlic starts to brown. Add onion, peppers, and okra and cook 2 minutes. Next add stock, rice, diced tomato, and bay leaf and bring to a boil. Reduce heat and simmer 30 to 40 minutes, stirring constantly. If needed, add more stock or water.

Check if rice is done. Add gumbo filé and adjust flavor with salt and pepper. Remove bay leaf before serving. Serve with hot sauce on the side.

Yield: 3 to 4 servings

Broccoli, Shrimp, and Cheddar Cheese Soup

The perfect soup for a cold, rainy afternoon. In this recipe you will prepare a broccoli-cheddar soup and garnish with shrimp.

2	*tablespoons* BUTTER
1	*head* BROCCOLI, *chopped (save 6 tiny florets for soup garnish and use remainder for stock)*
½	*cup* ONION, *chopped*
2	*tablespoons all-purpose* FLOUR
1	*quart* CHICKEN CONSOMMÉ
¼	*cup* HEAVY CREAM
¼	*pound* CHEDDAR CHEESE, *grated*
	SALT *and* PEPPER *to taste*
¼	*pound baby* SHRIMP, *cooked, peeled, and deveined*

Chop broccoli into small pieces (cook and save 6 florets for garnish). In a saucepan over moderate heat, combine butter and onion; cook until onion starts to become transparent. Add flour and stir until flour is dissolved. Next add chicken consommé and chopped broccoli; return to heat. Simmer for 20 minutes, stirring constantly or until broccoli is soft.

Pour mixture in blender or food processor. Purée until a smooth paste. Place back in saucepan. Add heavy cream and cheddar cheese. Simmer over low heat, making sure that cheese is melted. Stir often and do not burn pan. Adjust flavor with salt and pepper.

While soup is cooking, preblanch broccoli florets in a saucepan of boiling water. Chop shrimp into small pieces. When ready, add cooked shrimp and broccoli florets to soup and simmer for a couple of minutes.

Yield: 3 to 4 servings

Blue Marlin Sportfishing Chowder

A Floridian version of Manhattan chowder, but not quite as thick. With baseball and sportfishing sweeping Florida, what would cooking be like without blue marlin chowder?

¼	*cup* BACON, *chopped fine*
1	*teaspoon* GARLIC, *minced*

2   tablespoons PARSLEY, *chopped*

¼   ONION, *chopped*

½   *cup* RED BELL PEPPER, *chopped*

¼   *cup* CELERY, *chopped*

¼   *pound* BLUE MARLIN, *cut in small pieces for chowder*

1   *quart* FISH STOCK *or* CLAM JUICE *(see page 28)*

¼   *cup* LEEKS, *chopped (use only the white part)*

½   *medium* POTATO, *peeled and diced*

¾   *cup peeled, chopped* TOMATOES *in juice, canned*

½   *teaspoon* FENNEL SEED

1   BAY LEAF

¼   *teaspoon* THYME, *chopped*

     SALT *and* PEPPER *to taste*

1   *tablespoon* DARK JAMAICAN RUM

     HOT SAUCE *to taste*

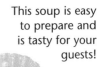

This soup is easy to prepare and is tasty for your guests!

Prepare fish stock or clam juice and set to the side.

In a large saucepan over moderate heat, combine bacon, garlic, parsley, onion, peppers, and celery. Cook until garlic starts to brown. Add blue marlin, stock, leeks, potatoes, tomatoes, fennel seed, bay leaf, thyme, salt, and pepper and simmer. Cook for 30 to 40 minutes. Skim top of chowder as needed.

When potatoes and vegetables are soft, add rum. Rum is not necessary but adds a nice touch. Cook 5 more minutes.

To serve, place Blue Marlin Sportfishing Chowder in individual serving bowls. Sprinkle excess chopped parsley on top for garnish. Remove bay leaf before serving. Serve with hot sauce on the side.

Yield: 2 servings

Seven Seas Onion Soup

Prized around the world for the magic it creates with its flavor and aroma, this subterranean bulb is a juicy specimen. When creating this soup, use onions that are in season for that extra-fresh, sweet taste.

2   tablespoons BUTTER

½   *tablespoon* GARLIC, *minced*

¼   YELLOW ONION, *chopped*

¼   RED ONION, *chopped*

¼   *cup* GREEN ONION, *chopped*

¼   cup LEEKS, *chopped (use only the white part)*
½   tablespoon SHALLOTS, *minced*
2   tablespoons GRANULATED SUGAR
¼   cup DRY SHERRY
3   cups CHICKEN CONSOMMÉ SOUP
1   *pinch of* WHITE PEPPER
⅛   teaspoon THYME, *chopped*
⅛   BAY LEAF
¼   cup HEAVY CREAM

Garnish

4   slices FRENCH BREAD
2   tablespoons CHIVES, *chopped*

Prepare garlic, yellow onion, red onion, green onion, and shallots for cooking. In saucepan over moderate heat, combine butter, garlic and onions, leeks, and shallots and sprinkle with sugar. Cook for 9 to 15 minutes (until tender and lightly brown), stirring constantly.

Onions come in two classifications: green, also called "scallions," and dry, which are covered with a dry, papery skin that surrounds juicy flesh.

Add sherry and simmer 1 minute. Next add chicken consommé, white pepper, thyme, and bay leaf. Bring to a boil, reduce to moderate heat, and simmer for 15 to 20 minutes. Skim top as needed.

Pour soup in blender or food processor and purée thoroughly. Return purée to pan and set over low heat. Whisk in heavy cream and simmer for 5 minutes.

Slice French bread and toast in oven broiler. Remove bay leaves before serving. Place soup in bowls and garnish with French bread and fresh chopped chives.

Yield: 2 servings

Famous Key West Conch Chowder with Dark Rum

A chowder that is as famous as the town itself.

½   pound CONCH, *ground*
¼   cup BACON, *chopped*
1   tablespoon GARLIC, *minced*
1   tablespoon PARSLEY, *chopped*
½   medium ONION, *chopped*

½ medium GREEN PEPPER, *chopped*
½ medium RED PEPPER, *chopped*
1 *cup* CELERY, *chopped*
¼ *cup fresh* FENNEL, *chopped*
¼ *cup fresh* LEEKS, *chopped*
2 *cups* CLAM JUICE
4 *cups* WATER
3 *tablespoons* LOBSTER BASE
1 *small* POTATO, *peeled and diced*
¼ *teaspoon* THYME
½ *teaspoon dry* FENNEL SEEDS
½ *teaspoon dry* ANISE SEEDS
   dash GUMBO FILÉ
¼ *teaspoon* TABASCO SAUCE
1½ *cups chopped* TOMATOES *in juice, canned*
¼ *cup* DARK JAMAICAN RUM

Grind or chop conch. In a large pan, fry bacon, conch, and parsley until lightly brown. Add onion, peppers, celery, fennel, and leeks; cook until vegetables are tender. Add clam juice, water, lobster base, potatoes, seasonings, and diced tomatoes. Cook about 40 minutes or until potatoes are tender. Add dark Jamaican rum and simmer 5 minutes. Serve hot.

Yield: 6 servings

Healthy Coleslaw

A tantalizing salad that complements seafood dishes perfectly.

½ *medium head of* CABBAGE, *cored and shredded*
½ *medium* CARROT, *grated*

Healthy Dressing
¼ *cup* CORN OIL
3 *tablespoons* RED WINE VINEGAR
1 *tablespoon* SUGAR
¼ *cup* RED BELL PEPPER, *chopped*
¼ *cup* RED ONION, *chopped*
1 *tablespoon fresh* DILL, *chopped*

In a small mixing bowl, thoroughly mix oil, vinegar, sugar, red pepper, red onion, and dill with a whisk. Adjust flavor with black pepper. Set to the side.

Shred cabbage. Place in mixing bowl and toss in grated carrot. Toss cabbage mix with Healthy Dressing. Chill coleslaw before serving.

Yield: 2 servings

Honey Mustard–Poppy Seed Coleslaw

Honey Mustard–Poppy Seed Coleslaw is sweet and tangy and is a great side dish. Goes with almost all seafood dishes!

½   *medium head* CABBAGE, *cored and shredded*
½   *cup* CARROT, *shredded*
      HONEY MUSTARD–POPPY SEED DRESSING (*see page 39*)

In a large mixing bowl, combine shredded cabbage and carrots. Toss with dressing until cabbage is thoroughly coated. Serve as a side dish with seafood entrées.

Yield: 2 servings

Grilled Eggplant and Sweet Potato

A tantalizing dish that is marinated, grilled, and served as a salad.

1   *large* SWEET POTATO
½   *medium* EGGPLANT

Balsamic Marinade
¼   *cup* VEGETABLE OIL
¼   *cup* BALSAMIC VINEGAR
1   *tablespoon* GARLIC, *minced*
½   LEMON, *squeezed for juice*
1   *teaspoon* BLACK PEPPER, *ground*

Garnish
      PARSLEY SPRIGS

In mixing bowl, combine ingredients listed for balsamic marinade and mix thoroughly. Set to the side.

Peel sweet potato and slice into ¼-inch-thick slices. Parboil the sweet potato slices for about 4 to 5 minutes. They should be slightly tender, yet al dente, so as to not fall apart when cooked on grill. Peel eggplant and slice into ¼-inch-thick slices. Add vegetables to Balsamic Marinade and let sit 30 to 40 minutes.

Preheat grill and, once hot, place vegetables on it. Grill vegetables on both sides until grill marks show and vegetables are cooked. Cooking time will vary depending on the type of vegetables and the heat level of the grill. When done, place on platter and dribble with extra marinade. Garnish with parsley sprigs.

Yield: 2 servings

Pineapple Boat with *Creamy Dill Shrimp Salad*

A real tropical beauty. The pineapple boat is great stuffed with shrimp salad and garnished with fresh fruit. Magnificent!

Creamy Dill Shrimp Salad

10	*ounces* SHRIMP, *medium or baby*
¼	*cup* MAYONNAISE
3	*tablespoons* CELERY, *chopped*
1	*tablespoon* ONION, *chopped*
¼	LEMON, *squeezed for juice*
1	*tablespoon* DILL, *chopped*
	SALT *and* PEPPER *to taste*

Presentation

1	*medium* PINEAPPLE
¼	*head* LEAF LETTUCE, *washed*
¼	CANTALOUPE, *peeled and diced*
½	*pint* STRAWBERRIES, *washed*
¼	*pint* RASPBERRIES, *washed*
2	*bunches* RED SEEDLESS GRAPES

Cook shrimp in a pot of boiling water. If using medium-size shrimp, it will take 1 to 2 minutes. When shrimp are done, remove from pot and cool with ice water. In mixing bowl, combine mayonnaise, celery, onion, lemon juice, and dill and mix thoroughly. Next, add shrimp and toss gently together. Add salt and pepper to taste.

Take the pineapple and split it in half lengthwise. If possible, also split the top in half. Cut out the inside of each pineapple half to form a boat. This is where you will place the Creamy Dill Shrimp Salad.

Now you will design the plate. First, cover plates with leaf lettuce, then set each half of pineapple on plates. The pineapple will be on one side of plate so fruit will sit in front. Fill each pineapple with shrimp salad. Clean and cut all fruit and arrange neatly in front of pineapple boats.

Yield: 2 servings

Caesar Salad with Blackened Pepper Shrimp

In this recipe, you will be making a classic Caesar dressing and home-made seasoned croutons to create a wonderful salad. To ensure a robust flavor from your shrimp, marinate them for two hours.

8	large SHRIMP, *peeled and deveined*
¼	tablespoon GARLIC, *minced*
¼	cup OLIVE OIL
I	LEMON, *squeezed for juice*
I	head ROMAINE LETTUCE
I	ripe TOMATO, *cored and cut into 8 pieces*
¼	cup PARMESAN CHEESE, *grated*

Classic Caesar Dressing (see page 40)

Homemade Garlic Croutons (see page 143)

Blackened Pepper Mix

½	teaspoon PAPRIKA
½	teaspoon ONION POWDER
½	teaspoon GARLIC POWDER
½	teaspoon ground WHITE PEPPER
½	teaspoon ground RED PEPPER
½	teaspoon ground BLACK PEPPER
½	teaspoon dried THYME, *crushed*

Garnish

    ANCHOVIES

Combine ingredients listed for the pepper mix in small bowl and mix thoroughly. Set to the side.

Peel and devein shrimp. To marinate shrimp, mix olive oil, garlic, lemon juice and ½ of Blackened Pepper Mix in a mixing bowl. Add peeled shrimp and marinate in refrigerator for 1 to 2 hours. Preheat grill and get ready to cook. Cook shrimp on grill on both sides for 2 to 3 minutes. When shrimp is cooked, place to the side.

Make Classic Caesar Dressing and Homemade Garlic Croutons.

Wash romaine lettuce and cut into bite-size pieces. The romaine can be precut early in the day and covered in the refrigerator. In large mixing bowl, add romaine, dressing, and croutons and mix thoroughly. On two dinner plates, place equal amounts of mixed romaine. Place shrimp and tomato pieces on top of salad. Sprinkle with Parmesan cheese and top with anchovies.

Yield: 2 servings

Sunshine Crabmeat Salad

A summertime salad great for a luncheon.

½	*pound* CRABMEAT
¼	*cup* MAYONNAISE *or* SALAD DRESSING
1	*tablespoon* ONION, *chopped*
½	*cup* CELERY, *chopped*
1	*tablespoon* SWEET PICKLE, *chopped*
1	HARD-COOKED EGG, *chopped*
¼	*teaspoon* SALT
	small dash WHITE PEPPER
1	*cup mixed* SALAD GREENS

Garnish

1	*ripe* TOMATO, *sliced*
2	BLACK OLIVES

Remove any shell or cartilage from crabmeat, being careful not to break the meat into small pieces. In large mixing bowl, combine all ingredients except lettuce, tomato, and black olives. Chill. Serve on lettuce. Garnish with tomato and black olives.

Yield: 2 servings

Royal Palm Lobster Salad with Mango Chutney and Papaya

Papaya, mixed with the sweet taste of lobster, will make this dish the talk of the town. The presentation is also a treat.

Mango Chutney and Papaya Mix

1	1- *to* 1 ½-*pound* LOBSTER, *Maine or Florida*
½	*large* PAPAYA, *ripe*
¼	*cup* MANGO CHUTNEY (*see page 33*)
¼	*cup* OLIVE OIL

½   *tablespoon* RED WINE VINEGAR

1   LIME, *squeezed for juice*

2   *tablespoons* RED ONION, *chopped*

2   *tablespoons fresh* BASIL, *chopped*

    pinch of ground BLACK PEPPER

Garnish

¼   *head* LEAF LETTUCE, *washed*

½   PAPAYA, *cut into 6 lengthwise slices*

4   STRAWBERRIES, *washed*

1   KIWI, *sliced*

    PARSLEY SPRIGS

In a large pot of boiling water, cook lobster for 8 to 10 minutes. When done, remove lobster and cool. Next split lobster lengthwise in half. Leave each half of shell unbroken. Remove all of the meat inside; if using Maine lobster, remove claw meat. Chop lobster meat and place in mixing bowl. Put empty lobster-shell halves to the side for later use.

A showboat salad!

Peel papaya, then split in half lengthwise; remove seeds and dice only one half. Half of the papaya is used for garnish and half is used for lobster-papaya mix. Place diced papaya in the mixing bowl containing the lobster. The other half of the papaya will be sliced lengthwise into thin slices and fanned on plate. In the mixing bowl containing the papaya and lobster, add chutney, olive oil, vinegar, lime juice, red onion, basil, and black pepper. Mix thoroughly, but gently.

Place lobster shells on one side of plate. Slice half of papaya in thin slices. Fan half on each plate, in front of lobster shell. Stuff each lobster shell with lobster-papaya mix. Slice strawberries in half and place on each plate. Garnish with kiwi slices and parsley sprigs.

Yield: 2 servings

"Old Floridian" Seafood Antipasto Platter

You will cook both entrées and appetizers for this recipe. This platter is served cold with roasted peppers and garlic.

1   ROASTED RED AND YELLOW BELL PEPPERS *(see page 131), one of each*

½   *recipe* LOBSTER CHUTNEY TRIANGLES *(see page 62)*

½   *recipe* MUSSELS AND CALAMARI TRI-PEPPER SALAD *(see below)*

½   *recipe* GALLERY SHRIMP WITH CRABMEAT STUFFING *(see page 123)*

1   *recipe* ROASTED GARLIC *(see page 131)*

1   *recipe* GRILLED EGGPLANT AND SWEET POTATO *(see page 70)*

Sauces

    LEMON COCKTAIL SAUCE *(see page 25)*

    FLORIDA PANTHER MUSTARD SAUCE *(see page 26)*

    RED REEF CORAL SAUCE *(see page 25)*

Garnish

¼   *head* LEAF LETTUCE, *washed*

    LEMON CROWNS, PARSLEY SPRIGS

Follow the recipes listed on the appropriate pages to prepare entrées and sauces. Cool hot food for this platter since it will be served cold.

Cover one large platter with leaf lettuce. Using three small sauce cups, place Lemon Cocktail Sauce, Florida Panther Mustard Sauce, and Red Reef Coral Sauce in the middle of platter.

Arrange all the food you prepared in a decorative and neat fashion on platters; garnish with lemon crowns and parsley sprigs. Serve family-style.

> The word "antipasto" usually suggests a plate of hors d'oeuvres.

Yield: 2 to 4 servings

Mussels and Calamari Tri-Pepper Salad

Aside from assembly, this salad can be prepared well in advance. There is an art to the preparation of crisp, cold salads. In this recipe, you will combine the flavors of seafood and vegetables seasoned to perfection.

¼   *pound* CALAMARI *meat, fresh or prepared*

12   MUSSELS

1   LEMON, *squeezed for juice*

½   *cup* OLIVE OIL

½   *tablespoon* GARLIC, *minced*

2   *tablespoons* RED WINE VINEGAR

½   RED, GREEN, *and* YELLOW BELL PEPPERS, *cut into julienne strips*

¼   RED ONION, *cut into thin strips*

6	PEPPERONCINIS, *chopped*
¼	*cup* BLACK OLIVES, *sliced*
1	LEMON, *squeezed for juice*
1	LIME, *squeezed for juice*
2	*tablespoons* CILANTRO, *chopped*
⅛	*teaspoon* TABASCO SAUCE
⅛	*teaspoon* BLACK PEPPER, *ground*

Garnish

1	*ripe* TOMATO
	LEMON CROWNS, PARSLEY SPRIGS

Clean and wash calamari; then slice tubes into rings. Wash mussels and pull off beards. In saucepan, boil water and add the juice of one lemon, calamari, and mussels. Cook for 1 to 2 minutes. Remove and cool down. In a medium mixing bowl, combine the remaining ingredients except garnish items and gently toss. Cover and let sit for 3 to 4 hours in refrigerator.

Place calamari and vegetables in middle of two plates. Place mussels on edge of plate for an artistic and scrumptious touch. Dribble with excess sauce as needed. Core and cut vine-ripe tomato into six wedges. Place tomato wedges on side of calamari mix, garnishing plates with lemon crowns and parsley sprigs.

Yield: 2 servings

Hurricane Seafood Salad with Black-Peppercorn Pasta

A blend of cooked seafood, marinated and placed on a chilled bed of homemade black-peppercorn pasta. A light meal in itself.

2	*ounces* FISH, *cut into small chunks*
2	*ounces* BAY SCALLOPS
2	*ounces* BABY SHRIMP
1	LEMON, *squeezed for juice*
⅛	*teaspoon* SALT
2	*ounces* CRABMEAT
¼	RED BELL PEPPER, *chopped*
½	*tablespoon* RED ONION, *chopped*
¼	*cup* GREEN ONIONS, *chopped*
¼	*cup* CELERY, *chopped*

½   *cup* CORN OIL

3   *tablespoons* RED WINE VINEGAR

½   LEMON, *squeezed for juice*

½   *tablespoon* DILL, *chopped*

1   *teaspoon* GRANULATED SUGAR

     SALT *and* PEPPER *to taste*

Black-Peppercorn Pasta (see page 146)

Garnish

2   SCALLION FLOWERS *(see page 130)*

     LEMON CROWNS, PARSLEY SPRIGS

Clean, cut, and prepare seafood for cooking. In a saucepan of boiling water, combine lemon juice and salt. Next add fish, scallops, and shrimp and cook for 3 minutes or until seafood is cooked. Strain and cool in refrigerator. In mixing bowl, combine peppers, onions, celery, oil, vinegar, lemon juice, fresh dill, and sugar. Mix thoroughly. Add seafood and crabmeat; gently toss. Adjust flavor with salt and pepper. Let sit 30 minutes in refrigerator.

Prepare Black-Peppercorn Pasta. Cook pasta and cool with ice water. When chilled, drain thoroughly.

When ready to serve, combine half of seafood mix with pasta, toss gently, and place on two plates. Place remaining seafood on top of pasta. Garnish with Scallion Flowers, lemon crowns, and parsley sprigs.

Yield: 2 servings

Lobster, Crab, and Alligator

Splitting Whole Lobsters

Lobsters should be split at the belly and cracked on the back, yet still in one piece (unless the recipe calls for the lobster to be split in half).

How to split lobsters: On a cutting board, place the lobster on its back. Using a French knife, thrust into the head and bring the knife down through the center of the lobster to split it in half (do not split lobster all the way through the back side). Using your hands, crack the back of the shell, spreading the lobster open. Clean out the stomach and vein in the lobster. The green tomalley can be added to the stuffing if you like. If using a Maine lobster, crack the claws with the back of the French knife.

Meat Yield

Northern Lobster

For the recipes requiring cooked northern lobster meat, cool lobsters after boiling and remove meat. Two live lobsters, 1 pound each, yield approximately ½ pound cooked lobster meat.

Rock or Spiny Lobster Tail

For recipes requiring cooked spiny lobster meat, cool tails after boiling and remove meat. One and one-half pounds of frozen lobster tails yield approximately ¾ pound cooked lobster meat.

How to Eat a Lobster

When serving northern lobster, wearing a bib is recommended while cracking claws. Fine restaurants will usually provide a small bowl of hot water and wet towel (or bev naps) for cleaning hands after dinner.

When eating a lobster served in the shell, use a small lobster or cocktail fork to remove the meat from the tail.

Use a lobster cracker or nutcracker to break the shell of the big claws.

Tasty chunks of solid meat are inside. Pull off each little claw and suck out the sweet tasty morsel of meat.

Recipes

Broiled Florida Lobster Tails

2   *5- to 8-ounce* FLORIDA SPINY LOBSTER TAILS

⅓   *cup* BUTTER *or* MARGARINE, *melted*

½   *teaspoon* SALT

     dash WHITE PEPPER

     dash PAPRIKA

¾   *cup* BUTTER *or* MARGARINE, *melted (for dipping)*

3   *tablespoons* LEMON JUICE

Cut lobster tails in half lengthwise. Lay lobster tails open as flat as possible on a broiler pan. Brush lobster meat with ⅓ cup of butter. Sprinkle with salt, pepper, and paprika. (To keep tails from curling while they broil, bend each tail backwards toward shell to crack). Broil about 4 inches from source of heat for 8 to 10 minutes, depending on size of lobster tails. Combine ¾ cup of butter and lemon juice in small saucepan; serve with lobster tails.

> Corn on the cob and melted butter wonderfully accompany any of the following lobster recipes!

Yield: 2 servings

Boiled Florida Spiny Lobster Tails

A quick and easy method for cooking lobster tails.

2   *5- to 8-ounce* FLORIDA SPINY LOBSTER TAILS

2   *quarts* BOILING WATER

⅓   *cup* SALT

     MELTED BUTTER

Place lobster tails in boiling salted water. Cover and return to boiling point. Simmer for 8 to 10 minutes, depending on size of lobster tails. Drain. (To keep tails from curling while they boil, bend each tail backwards toward shell to crack or insert skewer lengthwise between shell and meat). Cut in half lengthwise. Serve with melted butter.

Yield: 2 servings

Northern Broiled Lobster

Serve with corn on the cob and melted butter.

2	WHOLE LIVE LOBSTERS (*1 pound each*)
1	*tablespoon* BUTTER *or* MARGARINE, *melted*
¼	*teaspoon* SALT
	dash WHITE PEPPER
	dash PAPRIKA

Sauce

1	*cup* BUTTER *or* MARGARINE, *melted*
1	*tablespoon* LEMON JUICE

Garnish

LEMON CROWNS, PARSLEY SPRIGS

Side dish

2	CORNS ON THE COB, *cooked*

Place each live lobster on its back; insert a sharp knife between body shell and tail segment, cutting down to sever the spinal cord. Cut in half lengthwise. Remove the stomach, which is just behind the head, and intestinal vein, which runs from the stomach to the tip of the tail. Do not discard the green liver and coral roe; they are delicious. Crack the claws. (To keep tails from curling while they broil, bend each tail backwards toward shell to crack or place small heavy baking dish on end of tail to hold down.)

Lay lobsters open as flat as possible on a broiler pan. Brush lobster meat with butter. Sprinkle with salt, pepper, and paprika. Broil about 6 inches from source of heat for 10 to 12 minutes or until lightly browned. Combine butter and lemon juice; serve with lobsters. Garnish with parsley sprigs and lemon crowns.

Yield: 2 servings

Whole Boiled Northern Lobsters

In this recipe, you will boil whole lobsters and split, serve, or use meat for other recipes.

2	WHOLE LIVE NORTHERN LOBSTERS (*1 pound each*)
3	*quarts* BOILING WATER

3   *tablespoons* SALT
     MELTED BUTTER

Plunge lobsters head-first into boiling salted water. Cover and return to boiling point. Simmer for 8–10 minutes. Drain. (To keep tails from curling while they boil, insert skewer lengthwise between shell and meat.) Place each lobster on its back. With a sharp knife, cut in half lengthwise. Remove the stomach, which is just behind the head, and the intestinal vein, which runs from the stomach to the tip of the tail. Do not discard the green liver and coral roe; they are delicious. Crack the claws. Serve with butter.

Yield: 2 servings

Lobster Thermidor

A classic recipe that, when served in lobster shells, will look great and taste fantastic.

Preheat oven to 350°F.

2   WHOLE LIVE LOBSTERS *(1 pound each)*
2   *tablespoons* BUTTER *or* MARGARINE
2   *tablespoons all-purpose* FLOUR
½   *teaspoon* SALT
1½   *teaspoons* POWDERED MUSTARD
     dash CAYENNE PEPPER
1   *pint* HEAVY CREAM
1   *can (4 ounces)* MUSHROOM STEMS *and* PIECES, *drained*
¼   *cup* PARMESAN CHEESE, *grated*
¼   *teaspoon* PAPRIKA

Garnish
     LEMON CROWNS, PARSLEY SPRIGS

Split live lobsters lengthwise and remove meat (see page 78). Clean shells and rinse. Cut lobster meat into ½-inch pieces. Melt butter; blend in flour and seasonings. Gradually add cream and cook until thick and smooth, stirring constantly. Add mushrooms and lobster meat. Place in shells. Sprinkle with cheese and paprika. Place on a cookie sheet, 15½ x 12 inches. Bake in 350°F oven for 8 minutes or until brown.

Yield: 2 servings

Baked Stuffed Lobster with Ritz Cracker–Crabmeat Stuffing

This dish is made with Ritz Cracker–Crabmeat Stuffing, then baked to perfection.

Preheat oven to 350°F.

2	1- to 1½-pound LOBSTERS, *split and stomach cleaned out*

Ritz Cracker–Crabmeat Stuffing

3	*ounces* UNSALTED BUTTER
¼	ONION, *chopped*
¼	RED BELL PEPPER, *chopped*
¼	*cup* WHITE WINE
¼	LEMON, *squeezed for juice*
4	*ounces* CRABMEAT, *checked for shells*
2	*cups* RITZ CRACKERS, *crushed*
1	*tablespoon* PARSLEY, *chopped*

Sauce

CLARIFIED BUTTER *(see page 28)*

Garnish

LEMON CROWNS, PARSLEY SPRIGS

"Putting on the Ritz." Well, in this recipe you won't be putting on the ritz, but you will be putting Ritz Cracker stuffing into a lobster!

To make stuffing, in large sauté pan over moderate heat, add butter, onion, and red pepper, and cook for 5 minutes. Add wine and lemon juice, then cook 30 seconds. Add the crabmeat, crackers, and chopped parsley and gently fold together. Remove from heat.

See page 78 for instructions on splitting lobsters. On a baking sheet, place split lobster upside down and stuff the stomach with the Ritz Cracker–Crabmeat Stuffing mix. Do not cover up the tail meat. (To keep tails from curling while they broil, bend each tail backwards toward shell to crack or place small heavy baking dish on end of tail too hold down.) Brush tail with melted butter.

Bake lobsters at 350°F for 10 to 12 minutes or until done. Remove from oven and serve immediately. Serve with a small cup of Clarified Butter. Garnish with lemon crowns and parsley sprigs.

Yield: 2 servings

Lobster Lisa with a Sherry-and-Brandy Mornay Sauce

A classic dish that uses the flavors of sherry, brandy, and Parmesan cheese to enhance the flavor of lobster. For Phyllo Blossoms use phyllo dough, which is available in most supermarkets.

Preheat oven to 350°F.

Phyllo Blossoms
½	sheet PHYLLO DOUGH, *store-bought*
1	tablespoon OLIVE OIL

Lobster Lisa
½	ounce LOBSTER MEAT, *cut in medium-size pieces*
¼	cup SWEET SHERRY
¼	cup BRANDY
1	tablespoon CHIVES, *chopped*
	small pinch of WHITE PEPPER

Sauce
1	cup MORNAY SAUCE, *using only Parmesan cheese (see page 30)*

Garnish

LEMON CROWNS, PARSLEY SPRIGS

To make Phyllo Blossoms, cut phyllo sheet in half, then cut each half into six equal squares. Brush melted butter onto each phyllo square. Repeat until you have two stacks. Grease two 2½-inch muffin cup pans. Gently fit each stack into prepared muffin cups. Push down middle of blossom with the end of a cook's spoon. Bake 10 to 15 minutes at 350°F or until lightly browned. Remove from muffin cups and place on wire rack to cool.

In large sauté pan over moderate heat, combine olive oil and lobster meat. Sauté 1 to 2 minutes. Remove sauté pan 2 feet from stove to add sherry and brandy; using a long-handled match, ignite liquor (be careful of intensity of flame). Place back on stove. Next add white pepper, Mornay Sauce, and chives and cook until lobster meat is done.

Place blossom shells in center of plates with equal amount of lobster on each plate. Pour excess sauce on each plate and blossom shell. Garnish with lemon crowns and parsley sprigs.

Yield: 2 servings

Soft-Shell Crabs with Walnut-Orange Butter

This recipe is by far the easiest way to cook soft-shell crab. Soaking the crabmeat in herb milk will make it plump and juicy. Cooking the crab over moderate-high heat and in plenty of butter will make it crispy on the outside.

4	SOFT-SHELL CRABS, *cleaned*
1	*cup* MILK
1	*tablespoon* DRIED TARRAGON
½	*cup all-purpose* FLOUR
1	*tablespoon* PARSLEY, *chopped*
	SALT *and* PEPPER *to taste*
	OIL *for frying*

Walnut-Orange Butter

6	*ounces* BUTTER, *room temperature*
½	*tablespoon* TRIPLE SEC
1	*tablespoon* ORANGE JUICE, *concentrated*
1	*tablespoon* ORANGE RIND, *shredded*
2	*tablespoons* WALNUTS, *crushed fine*
1	*teaspoon* CHIVES, *chopped*
⅛	*teaspoon* ALLSPICE
	SALT *and* PEPPER *to taste*

Garnish

LEMON CROWNS, PARSLEY SPRIGS

To make Walnut-Orange Butter, thoroughly blend all ingredients listed in Walnut-Orange Butter mix in blender or food processor and set aside.

When you buy the crabs, ask the store to clean them for you. If not, begin by rinsing the live crabs thoroughly under cold water. Snip or cut off heads about ¼ inch behind the eyes (this will quickly kill the crabs). Then turn each crab on its back and lift or pull off the triangular apron on the lower part of shell. Flip crab over and peel back the points of the top shell and scrape out the gills on both sides. Rinse crab again and pat dry.

In a bowl large enough to hold the crabs laid out flat, place milk and tarragon leaves. Next, add crabs and let soak for 1 hour. Drain crabs and discard milk. Season the flour with parsley and salt and pepper and dredge each crab in seasoned flour. Heat oil in large sauté pan over moderate-high heat and place soft-shell crabs in single layers. Sauté 5 minutes on each side, or until crispy and golden brown. Place two crabs on each plate. On top of crabs, place Walnut-Orange Butter. Garnish with lemon crowns and parsley sprigs.

Yield: 2 servings

Stuffed Artichoke Boca-Style with Crabmeat

These artichokes are easy to prepare and present beautifully! Once cooked and dechoked (removing the tangles of hairs in the middle), they make a natural container for stuffing.

Preheat oven to 350°F.

2	large ARTICHOKES, *trimmed and precooked*

Crabmeat Stuffing

¼	cup OLIVE OIL
¼	cup ONION, *chopped*
1	tablespoon GARLIC, *minced*
1	cup WHITE BREAD CRUMBS, *fresh*
¼	cup CLAM JUICE *(see page 28)*
2	tablespoons FRESH BASIL, *chopped*
¼	teaspoon BLACK PEPPER
8	ounces JUMBO LUMP CRABMEAT *(check for shells)*
1	large EGG

Sauce

1	cup TOMATO-BASIL SAUCE *(see page 37)*

Garnish

ROMANO CHEESE, *grated*

LEMON WEDGES, PARSLEY SPRIGS

To make stuffing, in sauté pan over moderate heat, sauté olive oil, onion, and garlic, and cook for 5 to 8 minutes. Place mixture in mixing bowl, then add bread crumbs, clam juice, basil, black pepper, and crab-meat and blend thoroughly. In separate bowl, beat egg until fluffy and add to mix. Set aside.

Wash artichokes and cut 1 inch off the tops. Cut off stems, lower leaves, and pointers. Next, wrap in butcher twine. Cook artichokes by either boiling or steaming (instructions follow). Cook until three-fourths of the way done, remove, and let cool. Scrape out the fuzzy center from inside of choke with melon ball cutter.

Boiling Artichokes: Add lemon juice to water, bring to a boil, lower heat, and cook for 20 to 30 minutes.

Steaming Artichokes: Place sliced lemon on top of artichoke before tying. Steam for 30 to 40 minutes.

Using a spoon, take out inside of cooked and cooled artichoke and spread open. Fill cavity with crabmeat stuffing, also placing it between the outside leaves. Place stuffed artichokes in shallow baking pan and drizzle with remaining olive oil. Add 1 cup of water to pan, cover with tin foil, and bake at 350°F for 30 to 40 minutes. Next remove tin foil and sprinkle Romano cheese on top of artichokes; bake 10 more minutes. Remove artichokes from oven and serve with Tomato-Basil Sauce. Garnish with lemon wedges and parsley sprigs.

Yield: 2 servings

Homemade Crab Cakes with Panther and Cocktail Sauces

Homemade Crab Cakes, made with sweet lump crabmeat and served with mustard and cocktail sauces, make a special treat. This is an easy recipe that I enjoy making.

Homemade Crab Cakes

2	cups WHITE BREAD CRUMBS, *fresh*
8	ounces LUMP CRABMEAT, *checked for shells*
¼	cup CELERY, *chopped fine*
2	tablespoons ONION, *chopped fine*
¼	tablespoon all-purpose FLOUR
1	teaspoon OLD BAY SEASONING
⅛	teaspoon TABASCO SAUCE
	dash GINGER POWDER
1	*medium* EGG
¼	cup HELLMAN'S MAYONNAISE

¼   LEMON, *squeezed for juice*
    OIL, *for frying*

Sauces

FLORIDA PANTHER MUSTARD SAUCE *(see page 26)*
LEMON COCKTAIL SAUCE *(see page 25)*

Garnish

LEMON CROWNS, PARSLEY SPRIGS

Place bread in food processor to produce fluffy bread crumbs. Place in bowl and add crabmeat, celery, onion, flour, Old Bay, Tabasco, ginger, egg, mayonnaise, and lemon juice, and thoroughly blend. Portion crab mix into four even piles to form crab cakes. Mix should have a consistency that will hold together while forming and cooking. You may add more bread or liquid as needed.

In a large sauté pan over moderate heat, pour enough oil to coat bottom of pan. Now sauté crab cakes on both sides until golden brown. When done, place Homemade Crab Cakes on paper towels to drain. Serve immediately with Florida Panther Mustard Sauce and Lemon Cocktail Sauce. Garnish plates with lemon crowns and parsley sprigs.

Yield: 2 servings

Alligator à la Francaise with Fried Green Tomatoes

Truly a unique dish! Fried green tomatoes are a treat in themselves. But add alligator cooked French-style with Beurre Blanc Sauce and you will have a real winner.

10   *ounces* ALLIGATOR TENDERLOIN TAIL MEAT
2   *medium* GREEN TOMATOES
¼   *cup* OLIVE OIL
½   *cup all-purpose* FLOUR

Francaise Mix

2   *medium* EGGS
2   *tablespoons* PARMESAN CHEESE, *grated*
1   *tablespoon* PARSLEY, *chopped*

Sauce

BEURRE BLANC *(see page 27)*

Garnish

LEMON CROWNS, PARSLEY SPRIGS

To prepare Francaise mix, crack egg in mixing bowl and beat, then add Parmesan cheese and parsley. Whip thoroughly with a whisk.

Slice alligator meat, against the grain, into 6 portions. Pound into cutlets using meat mallet and plastic sheets. Slice green tomatoes into six ½-inch slices (do not use end pieces). Place to the side.

Add oil to a sauté pan over moderate heat. Coat green tomatoes in flour and fry until light golden brown on each side. Place on paper towel to drain. Coat alligator cutlets in flour and Francaise mix, then place in sauté pan and cook on both sides until lightly brown. Remove alligator and place on paper towels.

Place three fried green tomatoes on each plate, then Alligator Francaise, and pour Beurre Blanc over top. Garnish with lemon crowns and parsley sprigs.

Yield: 2 servings

Clams, Mussels, and Oysters

Shucking Hard Clams

The fishmonger or fish market will shuck clams for you if you ask. Wash the shell clams thoroughly, discarding any broken-shell or dead clams.

To open a hard clam, hold it in the palm of one hand with the shell's hinge against the palm. Insert a slender, strong, sharp knife between the halves of the shell and cut around the clam, twisting the knife slightly to pry open the shell. Cut both muscles free from the two halves of the shell. If the clam is to be served on the half shell, remove only one half of the shell. If it is to be used in one of the other recipes, remove and rinse the meat.

Since soft clams and surf clams do not have tight-fitting shells, they are easier to open. An alternate method is to place the shell clams, after washing, in a small quantity of boiling water. Cover and steam 5 to 10 minutes or until they are partially open. Drain, remove the meat from the shells, and wash the meat.

Purchasing Oysters

Oysters may be purchased in four forms: live in the shell, fresh shucked, frozen shucked, and canned.

Shell Oysters

Oysters in the shell are generally sold by the dozen and must be alive when purchased. When alive, they have a tightly closed shell. A gaping shell that does not close when handled indicates that the oyster is dead and therefore no longer usable. Be very careful when selecting shell oysters, as dead oysters can be quite poisonous.

Shucked Oysters

These are oysters that have been removed from the shell and are generally sold by the pint or quart. Shucked oysters should be plump and have a natural creamy color; they should also be free from shell pieces and have a clear liquor. Fresh shucked oysters are packed in metal containers or waxed cartons that should be refrigerated or packed on ice. When properly handled, they will remain fresh for up to ten days.

The Eastern oysters are generally packed in the following commercial grades:

Grade	Oysters per Gallon
Counts, or extra large	*No more than 160*
Extra selects, or large	*No more than 210*
Selects, or medium large	*No more than 300*
Standards, or small	*No more than 500*
Standards, or very small	*More than 500*

In recent years, shucked oysters have also been quick frozen, a process that makes them available year-round. Frozen oysters should not be thawed until ready to use. Once thawed, they should never be refrozen.

Canned Oysters

Canned oysters, packed on the Atlantic and Gulf Coasts, are usually sold in No. 1 Picnic Cans containing 7½ ounces of oysters in drained weight. Oysters packed on the Pacific Coast are usually sold in cans containing 5–8 ounces drained weight.

Quantity to Purchase

How the oysters are to be served largely determines the quantity of oysters that needs to be purchased. In purchasing oysters for six people, for example, you could purchase either three dozen shell oysters, one quart of shucked oysters, or two No. 1 cans.

Shucking Oysters

Wash and rinse the oysters thoroughly in cold water. Open or shuck an oyster by placing it on a table, flat shell up, and holding it with your left hand. With your right hand, force an oyster knife between the shell at or near the thin end. To make it easier to insert the knife, the thin end, or "bill," may be broken off with a hammer—a method preferred by some cooks. Now cut the large adductor muscle close to the flat upper shell in which it is attached and remove the shell. Cut the lower end of the same muscle, which is attached to the deep half of the shell. Leave the oyster loose in the shell if it is to be served on the half shell, or drop it into a container.

After shucking, examine the oysters for bits of shell, paying particular attention to the muscle, to which pieces of shell sometimes adhere. Instead of shucking by hand, a commercial mechanical oyster shucker is great to use if available.

Recipes

Key West Deviled Clams

The word "deviled" means that it tastes so devilishy good that you will like it.

Preheat oven to 350°F.

1	*pint* CLAMS
1	*tablespoon* MINCED GARLIC
2	*tablespoons* ONION, *chopped*
½	*cup* CELERY, *chopped*
¼	*cup* BUTTER *or* OTHER FAT, *melted*
1	*tablespoon all-purpose* FLOUR
¾	*teaspoon* SALT
¼	*teaspoon* WHITE PEPPER
¼	*teaspoon* THYME
3	*drops* TABASCO SAUCE
1	*tablespoon* CHILI SAUCE
1	EGG, *beaten*
½	*cup* CRACKER MEAL
2	*tablespoons* PARSLEY, *chopped*
2	*tablespoons* BUTTER *or* OTHER FAT, *melted*
½	*cups* DRY BREAD CRUMBS

Drain clams and save liquid. Cook garlic, onion, and celery in butter until tender. Blend in flour and seasonings. Add clams and their juice and cook until thick, stirring constantly. Stir the hot sauces and egg together and add to sauce in pan, stirring constantly. Add meal and parsley. Fill six well-greased individual shells or casseroles. Combine butter and crumbs; sprinkle over top of each shell. Bake at 350°F for 10 minutes or until brown.

Yield: 6 servings

Clam and Spinach Mornay

This recipe is cooked in a "casserole"—a term that defines a style of cooking and the baking dish in which it is cooked. Casserole dishes can be glass, metal, or ceramic, oven-proof and/or microwaveable. Bread crumbs and cheese are used as toppings for texture and flavor.

Preheat oven to 350°F.

16	CLAMS, *shucked, or 1 cup canned clams*
4	*ounces* SPINACH, *chopped*
1	*tablespoon* BUTTER
1	*tablespoon* GARLIC, *minced*
¼	RED ONION, *chopped*
2	*tablespoons* WHITE WINE
1	*teaspoon* TABASCO SAUCE
⅛	*teaspoon* BLACK PEPPER
¼	*pound* EGG NOODLES, *cooked*
¼	*cup* BREAD CRUMBS
1	*teaspoon* PAPRIKA

Sauce

1   *cup* MORNAY SAUCE *(see page 30)*

Prepare Mornay Sauce. Set to the side.

Shuck, wash, and chop clams. Wash spinach and pick off stems. In sauté pan over moderate heat, combine butter, garlic, and onion. Cook until garlic and onion start to become transparent. Reduce heat and add spinach and white wine, stirring constantly. Remove from heat and add clams, Mornay Sauce, Tabasco, and black pepper and set to the side. Cook pasta until three-quarters of the way done. Add egg noodles to Mornay-clam mix and blend thoroughly, yet gently.

Place mixture in casserole dish or baking dish and cover with bread crumbs and paprika. Bake 15 to 20 minutes at 350°F. Remove from oven and serve family-style.

Yield: 2 servings

Mussels Primavera with Almond-Cilantro Pesto

Pesto is an uncooked sauce made with fresh basil, garlic, pine nuts, Parmesan cheese, and olive oil. In this recipe you will substitute cilantro for basil and almonds for pine nuts. Cilantro has a flavor that fits well with highly seasoned food.

1   *pound* MUSSELS

2   *tablespoons* OLIVE OIL

1   CARROT, *peeled and julienned*

1   *head* BROCCOLI, *florets only*

½   ZUCCHINI, *diced*

½   RED ONION, *sliced thin*

2   RED BELL PEPPERS, *julienned*

    FETTUCCINE PASTA *(see page 146)*

Almond-Cilantro Pesto

¼   *cup* ALMONDS

1   *cup* OLIVE OIL

¼   *cup* PARMESAN CHEESE, *grated*

¼   *cup* CILANTRO, *chopped*

1   *tablespoon* GARLIC, *minced*

    SALT *and* WHITE PEPPER *to taste*

Garnish

LEMON CROWNS, PARSLEY SPRIGS

Prepare Fettuccine Pasta and set to the side.

To prepare Almond-Cilantro Pesto, place all ingredients listed for Almond-Cilantro Pesto in blender or food processor with metal blade. Blend thoroughly, pausing three or four times to scrape mixture down. Adjust flavor with salt and white pepper.

Clean mussels and wash thoroughly. Prepare vegetables for cooking and set to the side.

In sauté pan over moderate heat, combine mussels, olive oil, vegetables, and onion; sauté for 5 to 7 minutes. Next, add pesto and blend thoroughly. Cook until mussels open. Place pasta on two plates with mussels and vegetables on top and cover with any excess sauce. Garnish with lemon crowns and parsley sprigs.

Yield: 2 servings

Buttermilk-Cornmeal Fried Oysters

The oysters are soaked in buttermilk, breaded with cornmeal, and fried until golden brown. When deep frying, use fresh oil to ensure quality. Peanut oil is one of my favorites.

16   large OYSTERS, *shucked*

½   *cup* BUTTERMILK

½   *cup all-purpose* FLOUR

2   EGGS, *for egg wash (see below)*

¾   *cup* CORNMEAL

½   *tablespoon fresh* PARSLEY, *chopped*

      SALT *and* PEPPER *to taste*

      OIL, *for deep frying*

Lemon Cocktail Sauce (see page 25)

Garnish

LEMON CROWNS, PARSLEY SPRIGS

Side dish

HEALTHY COLESLAW *(see page 69)*

Prepare Lemon Cocktail Sauce and Healthy Coleslaw and place in refrigerator until needed.

Shuck oysters and soak in buttermilk for 3 to 4 hours to enhance flavor. Next, coat oysters in flour and egg wash. Combine cornmeal, parsley, salt, and pepper, then place oysters in mix and coat evenly. (See Standard Breading Procedure below.)

This is a classic recipe that is served with cocktail sauce.

In a deep sauté pan, heat oil over moderate heat and add oysters. Fry on both sides until light golden brown. Remove and place oysters on paper towel to drain. Serve with Lemon Cocktail Sauce and Healthy Coleslaw. Garnish with lemon crowns and parsley sprigs.

Yield: 2 servings

Standard Breading Procedure:

Breading refers to coating a product with bread crumbs, flour, cornflakes, or cornmeal before deep-frying, pan-frying, or sautéing. The following is the standard procedure for breading:

Step one: flour

Step two: egg wash—whole egg, or yolk, mixed only with a small amount of water or milk

Step three: breading

Oysters Palm Beach with Balsamic Hot Bacon Sauce

If you like oysters, then you'll love this dish! In this recipe, you will use exquisite balsamic vinegar. A treasure of a treat when combined with onion, bacon, and other fresh ingredients to create Oysters Palm Beach!

16	large OYSTERS, *shucked*
1	tablespoon OLIVE OIL
2	slices BACON, *diced*
½	RED ONION, *sliced thin*
½	tablespoon GARLIC, *minced*
2	LEEKS, *cut julienne-style*
¼	cup WHITE WINE
¼	cup BALSAMIC VINEGAR
2	tablespoons fresh BASIL, *chopped*
1	tablespoon CHIVES, *chopped*
	SALT *and* PEPPER *to taste*
8	ounces BASIL FETTUCCINE PASTA (*see page 146*)

Sauce

1	cup CLAM VELOUTÉ (*see page 29*)

Garnish

LEMON CROWNS, PARSLEY SPRIGS

Make Basil Fettuccine Pasta. Set the uncooked pasta to the side.

Shuck and wash oysters. In sauté pan, combine olive oil, bacon, and onion and cook over moderate heat until onion starts to lightly brown. Add garlic, leeks, and oysters and cook for 2 to 3 minutes. Add white wine and balsamic vinegar and reduce liquid by half. Add Clam Velouté, basil, and salt and pepper; cook for 3 minutes.

Cook Basil Fettuccine Pasta in a saucepan of boiling water. To serve, place oysters with sauce over two beds of pasta. Sprinkle chives on top. Garnish with lemon crowns and parsley sprigs.

Yield: 2 servings

Flat and Round Fish

Crusty Almond-Coated Mako Shark with Margarita Butter

Crusty! Remember that word when preparing this dish. In this recipe, fish is breaded with a mixture of cornmeal and slivered almonds. It is then sautéed until crusty and crispy and served with Margarita Butter for extra flavor.

16	ounces MAKO SHARK FILLETS, *boneless*
½	cup all-purpose FLOUR
1	EGG, *for egg wash (see page 94)*
½	cup CORNMEAL
½	cup BREAD CRUMBS
¼	cup SLIVERED ALMONDS
3	tablespoons VEGETABLE OIL

Margarita Butter

4	ounces WHOLE BUTTER, *at room temperature*
½	LEMON, *squeezed for juice*
½	LIME, *squeezed for juice*
2	tablespoons TRIPLE SEC
1	tablespoon fresh PARSLEY, *chopped*

Garnish

KOSHER SALT

LEMON *and* LIME, *sliced*

PARSLEY SPRIGS

To prepare Margarita Butter, add room-temperature butter, lemon and lime juice, Triple Sec, and parsley to mixing bowl; blend thoroughly. Set aside.

Cut Mako shark fillets into ½-inch thick slices, about 3 per serving. Coat shark in flour, then place in egg wash. Coat thoroughly with mixture of cornmeal, bread crumbs, and slivered almonds.

In preheated, large sauté pan over moderate heat, combine oil and fish, then sauté until golden brown and crispy, about 3 to 4 minutes on each side. Remove and place on plates.

Melt Margarita Butter in a sauté pan. Be sure to stir often so the butter does not burn. Drizzle Margarita Butter over the shark and sprinkle kosher salt on each end. Garnish with lemon and lime slices and parsley sprigs.

Yield: 2 servings

Halibut Steaks with Paradise Green Sauce

This recipe uses a combination of spices that will suit almost any fish. Try it and believe! In creating the sauce, you will use a blender or food processor to release the flavors of the green vegetables.

Preheat oven to 325°F.

2	*8-ounce* HALIBUT *steaks*
¼	*cup* MELTED BUTTER
¼	*cup* DRY WHITE WINE

Paradise Green Sauce

½	*cup* CELERY, *chopped*
¼	*cup* GREEN PEPPER, *chopped*
¼	*cup* GREEN ONIONS, *chopped*
¼	*cup* WATERCRESS
¼	*cup* DRY WHITE WINE
2	*tablespoons fresh* BASIL, *chopped*
1	*tablespoon* GRANULATED SUGAR
2	*tablespoons* OLIVE OIL
2	*tablespoons* RICE VINEGAR
1	*teaspoon* GARLIC, *minced*
½	*teaspoon fresh* GINGER, *peeled*
1	LIME, *squeezed for juice*
1	LEMON, *squeezed for juice*

Garnish

LIME CROWNS, PARSLEY SPRIGS

To prepare Paradise Green Sauce, combine ingredients listed for Paradise Green Sauce in an blender or food processor and purée for 1 to 2 minutes, pausing three times to scrape down the sides of the bowl.

Pour out into small mixing bowl.

Place halibut in a greased baking pan. Cover each piece of halibut with an even coat of Paradise Green Sauce. Add melted butter and white wine to give fish added flavor. Refrigerate at least 3 hours.

Bake fish at 375°F until a light, golden color starts to form, about 12 to 14 minutes. Remove fish from oven and place on plates. Pour extra sauce from baking pan on top of halibut. Garnish with lime crowns and parsley sprigs.

Yield: 2 servings

Poached Red Snapper with Orange-Tarragon Sauce

Red snapper, when poached, is very delicate, so it must be handled carefully! Its flesh is firm and has very little fat to hold it together. In this recipe, you will poach the fish in a citrus-based marinade and serve with a tangy sauce that your guests will rave about!

2	*8-ounce* RED SNAPPER FILLETS, *boneless and skinless*
4	ORANGES, *squeezed for juice*
1	CARROT, *julienned (see page 130)*
2	CELERY STICKS, *julienned*
½	ONION, *sliced thin*
½	*cup* DRY WHITE WINE
2	*tablespoons* TARRAGON VINEGAR
	WATER *for poaching fish*
	ORANGE-TARRAGON SAUCE *(see page 36)*

Garnish

ORANGE, *sliced*

TARRAGON SPRIGS

Prepare Orange-Tarragon Sauce. Keep warm and set to the side.

In a saucepan large enough to allow the snapper fillets to lay flat, combine orange juice, carrot, celery, onion, white wine, vinegar, and water. (There should be sufficient water to cover fish when added). Bring water to a boil.

Reduce heat and add red snapper, making sure fillets lay flat. Poach in flavored water for 8 to 12 minutes or until cooked. When removing snapper, be careful, as the fish will be tender and soft. Drain off excess water.

Place snapper on two plates. Drain vegetables and place on top of fish. Drizzle with Orange-Tarragon Sauce. Garnish with orange slices and tarragon sprigs.

Yield: 2 servings

Baked Flounder with Lemon-Dill Dressing

Flounder is a prized species of fish known for its fine texture and delicate flavor. Using this recipe, you will learn to prepare a seasoned, cooked dressing that is blended with crackers. This dressing will smother the flounder and bake it to perfection.

Preheat oven to 350°F.

½	cup SALTINE CRACKERS, *crushed fine*
2	8-ounce FLOUNDER *fillets, boneless and skinless*
2	teaspoons PAPRIKA
¼	cup MELTED BUTTER
¼	cup DRY WHITE WINE
1	LEMON, *squeezed for juice*

Sauce

LEMON-DILL DRESSING (*see page 41*)

Garnish

LEMON CROWNS, PARSLEY SPRIGS

Prepare Lemon-Dill Dressing. Finely crush saltine crackers and thoroughly blend with Lemon-Dill Dressing in mixing bowl.

Grease the bottom of a shallow baking pan and add flounder fillets. Cover each piece of flounder with an even coat of the cracker-and-dressing mix. Sprinkle with paprika for color. Add melted butter, white wine, and lemon juice to fish to add flavor while cooking. Bake fish at 350°F until golden brown or until fish is done. Remove fish from oven and place on two plates. Garnish with lemon crowns and parsley sprigs.

Yield: 2 servings

Grilled Salmon with Honey-Mustard Glaze and Rutabagas

Fresh salmon is an integral part of some of the world's most famous recipes. Rutabaga is a cabbage family root about 3 to 5 inches in diameter, which has a pale yellow skin and a sweet, firm flesh of the same color. In this recipe, you'll grill the salmon with a honey mustard glaze and add julienned rutabaga to create a magnificent dish!

Preheat grill to moderate temperature.

16	ounces SALMON FILLETS, *boneless and skinless*
1	RUTABAGA, *peeled and julienned (see page 130)*
2	*tablespoons* VEGETABLE OIL
1	*teaspoon* GARLIC, *minced*
¼	*cup* DRY WHITE WINE
¼	LEMON, *squeezed for juice*

Honey-Mustard Glaze

½	*cup* DIJON MUSTARD
½	*cup* HONEY
⅓	*cup* MAYONNAISE
⅛	*teaspoon ground* BLACK PEPPER

Garnish

LEMON CROWNS, PARSLEY SPRIGS

To prepare Honey-Mustard Glaze, blend ingredients in small mixing bowl. Mix into a smooth paste. Set to the side.

Rub salmon with 1 tablespoon of oil and place on grill heated to a moderate temperature. Marinate both sides of salmon with the Honey-Mustard Glaze while the fish is cooking. Salmon should take 4 to 6 minutes on each side to grill.

Peel rutabagas and cut julienne style. In sauté pan over moderate heat, combine 1 tablespoon oil, rutabagas, and garlic; cook for 2 minutes. Add white wine and lemon juice and cook for 2 minutes. Remove from heat, cover, and set aside.

Place equal amounts of drained rutabagas on two plates. Place fish on top and dribble with extra sauce. Garnish with lemon crowns and parsley sprigs.

Yield: 2 servings

Pompano Macadamia with Papaya Beurre Blanc

The mild and exquisite taste of macadamia is well worth the expense.

2	*6-ounce* POMPANO FILLETS, *boneless and skinless*
⅓	*cup all-purpose* FLOUR

1   EGG, *for egg wash*

¼   *cup* WHITE BREAD CRUMBS, *freshly chopped in food processor*

3   *ounces* MACADAMIA NUTS, *chopped in food processor*

¼   *cup* VEGETABLE OIL

Papaya Beurre Blanc (see page 27)

Garnish

½   PAPAYA, *peeled and sliced*

    LIME, *sliced*

    PARSLEY SPRIGS

Prepare Papaya Beurre Blanc and set aside.

Coat pompano with flour. Place in egg wash and set to the side. Mix the chopped macadamia nuts and white bread crumbs in a bowl. Remove pompano from egg wash and coat in bread-nut mix; coat fish on both sides. Pat on more bread crumbs and nut mix to secure a nice thick coat on fish.

Heat vegetable oil over moderate heat in a sauté pan. Add pompano and sauté on both sides until light golden brown. Remove fish from heat and place on plates.

Dribble Papaya Beurre Blanc around pompano. Garnish with sliced papaya, lime, and parsley sprigs.

Yield: 2 servings

Atlantic Pompano en Papillote

Pompano, a member of the Jack family, is found in the waters off the south Atlantic and Gulf states. In this recipe, you'll learn the art of steaming fish in a paper bag, a method that seals in flavor.

Preheat oven to 350°F.

12   *ounces* POMPANO FILLETS, *boneless*

2   *large pieces parchment paper*

½   *cup* VEGETABLE OIL

3   *tablespoons* BUTTER

½   LEEK, *julienned*

1   RED PEPPER, *julienned*

¼   RED ONION, *julienned*

4   MUSHROOMS, *sliced*
2   *tablespoons* DRY SHERRY
    SALT *and* PEPPER *to taste*

Garnish

LEMON CROWNS, PARSLEY SPRIGS

In sauté pan over moderate heat, combine butter, leek, pepper, onion, and mushrooms and cook 6 to 7 minutes. Add sherry and simmer 1 minute. Remove from heat and adjust flavor with salt and pepper.

To cook fish in parchment paper, follow these instructions. (Note: Aluminum foil may be used instead of parchment.) Fold paper in half and cut out half a heart from the folded side. The heart must be big enough to hold the fish and vegetables and leave room to crimp the edges.

Oil both sides of parchment. Place pompano on one side of the heart as shown. Cover with sautéed vegetables, drizzle with sauce, then fold over the other half of the heart.

Starting at the top of the fold, make a small crimp in the edge. Continue crimping around the edges. As you crimp, hold the previous crimp in place. When you reach the bottom of the heart, fold the point under to hold it in place. The Atlantic Pampano en Papillote is now ready to cook.

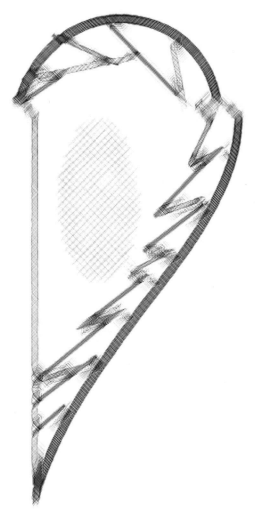

Bake the fish at 350°F for 10 to 13 minutes or until fish is cooked. Note: Pompano is a thin fish, and it will cook fast. Remove from oven and place fish on plates. Garnish and serve immediately. (When opening parchment, be careful not to burn yourself on the steam.)

Yield: 2 servings

Orange Roughy with Mango-Pepper Relish

Preheat oven to 350°F.

2	8-oz. ORANGE ROUGHY FILLETS, *boned and skinned*
¼	*cup* BUTTER, *melted*
1	*teaspoon* PAPRIKA
½	*teaspoon* PARSLEY, *chopped*
½	*cup* DRY WHITE WINE
	SALT *and* WHITE PEPPER *to taste*
	LEMON, *squeezed for juice*

Mango-Pepper Relish

½	*cup ripe* MANGO, *diced*
¼	*cup* RED BELL PEPPER, *diced*
¼	*cup* GREEN BELL PEPPER, *diced*
¼	*cup* OLIVE OIL
¼	LIME, *squeezed for juice*
3	*tablespoons* RICE VINEGAR
2	*tablespoons fresh* BASIL, *chopped*
	SALT *and* WHITE PEPPER *to taste*

Garnish

LEMON CROWNS, PARSLEY SPRIGS

> Mango-Pepper Relish can be used for chicken as well as fish.

To prepare Mango-Pepper Relish, toss together the ingredients listed for Mango-Pepper Relish in a bowl.

Grease the bottom of a shallow baking pan and place orange roughy fillets inside. Brush top with butter, then sprinkle paprika and parsley on top in an even coat. Add melted butter, white wine, and lemon juice.

Bake fish at 350°F until light golden brown or until fish is done, about 8–12 minutes. Remove fish from oven and place on two plates. Serve with Mango-Pepper Relish. Garnish with lemon crowns and parsley sprigs.

Yield: 2 servings

Grilled Tuna with Roasted Pepper Coulis

Tuna has a rich-flavored flesh that is firmly textured yet flaky and tender. Tuna is best when cooked medium-rare to rare, as this keeps it from drying out. Roasted Red and Yellow Pepper Coulis is the perfect sauce to accompany this tender fish.

Preheat grill.

- 1   *12-ounce* TUNA FILLET, *skinless and boneless*
- 1   *cup* OLIVE OIL
- 1   *tablespoon* GARLIC, *minced*
- 1   *tablespoon cracked* BLACK PEPPER
- 1   LEMON, *squeezed for juice*

Roasted Red and Yellow Pepper Coulis (see page 49)

Garnish
- 2   TARRAGON *leaves*
    LEMON CROWNS

Separately, prepare Roasted Red Pepper Coulis and Yellow Pepper Coulis. Do not mix the colors. Set to the side.

Cut tuna into two pieces. Marinate fillets in olive oil, garlic, black pepper, and lemon juice for 1 hour. Place tuna on hot grill and cook 3 to 4 minutes per side. Tuna should always be cooked slightly medium-rare, like roast beef. Remove from grill when done.

Take each fillet of grilled tuna and cut 4 to 5 slices against the grain. Fan out on plates. Pour a small amount of Red Pepper Coulis and Yellow Pepper Coulis on each side of fanned-out tuna. Garnish with tarragon leaves and lemon crowns.

Yield: 2 servings

Dolphin with "Old Floridian" Grill Seasoning

Dolphin, a saltwater fish, is also known as Mahi Mahi. The seasoning used is an old Greek recipe from the Florida Keys.

Preheat grill.

- 2   *9-ounce* DOLPHIN FILLETS, *boneless and skinless*
- ¼   *cup* OLIVE OIL
- 1   *tablespoon fresh* GARLIC, *minced*
- 1   LEMON, *squeezed for juice*

"Old Floridian" Grill Seasoning
- 4   *tablespoons* PAPRIKA
- 2   *tablespoons* GARLIC SALT

1	*tablespoon* ONION SALT
1	*tablespoon* GARLIC POWDER
1	*tablespoon* ONION POWDER
1	*tablespoon dry* BASIL
½	*tablespoon dry* OREGANO
½	*tablespoon dry* TARRAGON
1	*teaspoon ground* GINGER
¼	*teaspoon dry* THYME
½	*teaspoon* WHITE PEPPER
⅛	*teaspoon* CUMIN

Red and Yellow Tomato-Cilantro Salsa (see page 42)

Garnish

SUN-DRIED TOMATO COULIS *(see page 48)*
LEMON CROWNS, PARSLEY SPRIGS

Combine all ingredients listed in "Old Floridian" Grill Seasoning. Blend thoroughly.

Prepare Red and Yellow Tomato-Cilantro Salsa; cover and refrigerate until ready to serve.

In medium-size bowl, mix olive oil, garlic, lemon juice, and half of "Old Floridian" Grill Seasoning. Marinate fish in the mixture for at least an hour, 30 minutes on each side. Place dolphin fillets on preheated grill and cook for 4 to 6 minutes on each side, basting with leftover marinade and "Old Floridian" Grill Seasoning.

When fish is done, place on plates and serve with Red and Yellow Tomato-Cilantro Salsa. Garnish with lemon crowns and parsley sprigs.

When ready to serve seafood, use Sun-Dried Tomato Coulis and the painting techniques found on pages 45–6 to create designs on top of seafood and plate. Always paint the plates right before serving.

Yield: 2 servings

"Islamorada" Yellowtail Snapper with Creamy Bourbon Sauce

In this recipe, you will be using an all-American liquor named after Bourbon County, Kentucky. You will burn the liquor out of the bourbon to create the sauce. Use caution when preparing this tasty, flammable dish!

2	9-ounce YELLOWTAIL FILLETS, *boneless and skinless*
¼	cup all-purpose FLOUR
2	tablespoons VEGETABLE OIL
2	tablespoons SHALLOTS, *minced*
1	tablespoon BUTTER
¼	cup BOURBON
¼	cup HEAVY CREAM
1	tablespoon BASIL, *chopped*
½	LIME, *squeezed for juice*
⅛	teaspoon ground BLACK PEPPER
1	cup CLAM VELOUTÉ (*see page 29*)

Garnish

LIME, *sliced*

PARSLEY SPRIGS

Heat oil in sauté pan over moderate heat. Coat yellowtail in flour and place in hot sauté pan. Sauté on each side until fish browns. Remove yellowtail from pan, place to the side, and prepare sauce.

Add shallots and 1 tablespoon of butter; sauté for 2 minutes. Move sauté pan 2 feet from stove. Add bourbon, and, using a long-handled match, light liquor (be careful of intensity of flame). Place back on stove.

Next, add heavy cream and reduce by half. Add Clam Velouté, basil, lime juice, and black pepper. Stir mixture constantly, adding more cream if sauce is too thick after cooking. Place yellowtail back in pan and finish cooking until done.

Remove fish and place on two plates. Dribble extra sauce on top. Garnish with lime slices and parsley sprigs.

Yield: 2 servings

Swordfish Kabobs with Orange-Pecan Barbecue Sauce

This is a recipe that you have to try at your next barbecue party! Swordfish is the perfect fish for kabobs, because it has a mild flavor, firm flesh, dense meat, and will hold to skewers well. With a medley of vegetables and an extraordinary barbecue sauce, this is a treasure of a treat!

1	16-ounce SWORDFISH FILLET, *skinless and boneless, cut into 12 cubes*
½	ONION, *cut into medium-size pieces*
2	MUSHROOMS, *washed*

½   RED BELL PEPPER, *cut into medium-size pieces*

½   GREEN BELL PEPPER, *cut into medium-size pieces*

Yellow Saffron Rice (see page 140)

Sauces

ORANGE-PECAN BARBECUE SAUCE *(see page 35)*

CLASSIC HERB-CITRUS MARINADE *(see page 23)*

Garnish

ORANGE TWIST

PARSLEY SPRIGS

Prepare Orange-Pecan Barbecue Sauce and set to the side.

To prepare kabobs, cut swordfish and vegetables. Thread equal amounts of swordfish, onion, mushrooms, and peppers onto two skewers.

Prepare Classic Herb-Citrus Marinade. Marinate swordfish kabobs for 1 hour.

Preheat grill. When grill is hot, cook swordfish kabobs. Baste with Orange-Pecan Barbecue Sauce while kabobs are cooking. Remove kabobs and serve on bed of Yellow Saffron Rice. Serve extra barbecue sauce on the side. Garnish with parsley sprigs and orange twist.

Yield: 2 servings

Baked Bluefish with Fu Fu Crumbs and Avocado-Mango Relish

"Fu Fu" is a kitchen term that refers to a bread crumb mix that is used for cooking seafood in Florida restaurants. This is an old-time classic I learned at the Boca Raton Hotel and Resort.

Preheat oven to 325°F.

2   *8-ounce* BLUEFISH FILLETS, *boneless and skinless*

¼   *cup* BUTTER, *melted*

¼   *cup* DRY WHITE WINE

LEMON *squeezed for juice*

Fu Fu Bread Crumbs

½   *cup* DRY BREAD CRUMBS

2   *tablespoons* MELTED BUTTER

1   teaspoon PAPRIKA
½   teaspoon PARSLEY, *chopped*
     SALT *and* PEPPER *to taste*

Avocado-Mango Relish
½   cup ripe AVOCADO, *diced*
½   cup ripe MANGO, *diced*
2   tablespoons OLIVE OIL
¼   LIME, *squeezed for juice*
2   tablespoons RICE VINEGAR
1   tablespoon BASIL, *chopped*
     SALT *and* PEPPER *to taste*

Garnish
    MANGO-WASABI COULIS (*see page 47*)
    LEMON CROWNS, PARSLEY SPRIGS

To make Fu Fu Bread Crumbs, blend bread crumbs, butter, paprika, and parsley in mixing bowl. Adjust flavor with salt and pepper and mix thoroughly. If using fresh bread, place in oven at 225°F for 30 minutes to dry out. Put in food processor and purée into crumbs. Set to the side.

To prepare Avocado-Mango Relish, combine ingredients listed for relish in a mixing bowl and toss thoroughly. Set to the side.

Grease the bottom of a shallow baking pan and add bluefish fillets. Cover each piece of fish with an even coat of the Fu Fu Bread Crumbs. Next add melted butter, white wine, and lemon juice to give fish flavor while cooking.

Bake fish at 325°F until light golden brown or until fish is done, about 8 to 12 minutes. Remove fish from oven and place on two plates. Serve with Avocado-Mango Relish. Garnish with lemon crowns and parsley sprigs.

Prepare coulis ahead of time and place in squeeze bottle to be served at room temperature. When ready to serve seafood, use Mango-Wasabi Coulis and painting techniques on pages 45–6 to create designs on top of seafood and plate. Always paint the plates immediately before serving seafood.

Yield: 2 servings

Stuffed Dolphin Florentine with Creamy Artichoke Sauce

Dolphin is a moderately flat fish with firm flesh. Stuffing dolphin is unique, as dolphin is one of the few fish you can lightly pound out, stuff, and roll like a heavy tortilla. Once you get the technique down, you can stuff dolphin with any of your favorite ingredients.

Preheat oven to 350°F.

2	8-oz. DOLPHIN FILLETS, *with no bones, skin, or vein lines*
1	ROASTED RED PEPPER *(see page 131)*
¼	*cup* BREAD CRUMBS
¼	*cup* MELTED BUTTER
½	*cup* DRY WHITE WINE
1	LEMON, *squeezed for juice*

Florentine Stuffing Mix

8	*ounces fresh* SPINACH
1	*ounce* BUTTER
2	*tablespoons* GARLIC, *minced*
¼	*cup* ONION, *chopped*
¼	*cup* DRY WHITE WINE
1	LEMON, *squeezed for juice*
¼	*cup* HEAVY CREAM
2	*tablespoons* PARMESAN CHEESE, *grated*

Creamy Artichoke Sauce (see page 30)

Garnish

LEMON CROWNS, PARSLEY SPRIGS

To prepare Florentine Stuffing Mix, thoroughly wash spinach and remove the stems. In sauté pan over moderate heat, combine butter, garlic, onion, and spinach. Cook until spinach is reduced. Add white wine and reduce by half. Add heavy cream and lemon juice; reduce until liquid is almost evaporated from pan. Remove from heat, add Parmesan cheese, and mix thoroughly. Remove from sauté pan and set to the side.

Stuffing the dolphin fillets: Place dolphin fillets on cutting board and cover with a piece of plastic. Using a meat mallet, lightly pound out the fish (do not pound too hard; keep fillet in one piece). Remove plastic. Place Florentine Stuffing in the middle of each dolphin fillet. Place slice of red pepper lengthwise in middle. Take one edge of fillet and fold up over stuffing mix. Keep folding and roll over to close dolphin. Tuck in ends.

Prepare Creamy Artichoke Sauce. Set to the side.

Grease the bottom of a shallow baking pan and place the stuffed dolphin fillets inside. Sprinkle with bread crumbs and dribble with melted butter to moisten. Add white wine and lemon juice to pan (not over bread crumbs).

Bake dolphin at 350°F for 10 to 12 minutes or until done. Test inside of dolphin with a fork to see if done. Remove from oven.

Slice dolphin at an angle into four pieces and carefully lay them out on plates to form a fan. Place Artichoke Sauce on plate around dolphin. Garnish with lemon crowns and parsley sprigs and serve.

Yield: 2 servings

Multi-Seafood Dishes

Classic Seafood Stew with Old-Fashioned Herb Dumplings

The natural juices of fresh seafood, when properly combined with other ingredients, will create a most delicious stew!

8	ounces SNAPPER FILLETS, *boneless and skinless*
6	medium SHRIMP, *peeled and deveined*
¼	pound SEA SCALLOPS, *clean of muscle*
6	MUSSELS, *washed and debearded*
6	CLAMS, *washed*
1	tablespoon OLIVE OIL
1	teaspoon GARLIC, *minced*
½	CARROT, *julienned (see page 130)*
2	sticks CELERY, *julienned*
¼	RED ONION, *sliced thin*
¼	cup LEEK, *julienned*
4	MUSHROOMS, *cut in quarters*
½	cup VERMOUTH *or* DRY WHITE WINE
½	LEMON, *squeezed for juice*
1	tablespoon fresh CHIVES, *chopped*

Old-Fashioned Herb Dumplings (see page 142)

Sauce

2	cups CLAM VELOUTÉ *(see page 29)*

Prepare Old-Fashioned Herb Dumplings. Cook dumplings and cool; reheat when needed.

Cut fish fillet into two pieces and prepare seafood for stew as directed. Prepare vegetables as directed.

In saucepan over moderate heat, combine olive oil, garlic, and vegetables and sauté for 3 to 4 minutes. Add seafood; cook for 4 minutes, stirring constantly. Add vermouth and reduce juices by half. Add Clam Velouté and lemon juice, cover sauce pot, and lower heat. Simmer 8 to

10 minutes. While seafood is cooking, reheat dumplings.

Divide seafood mix evenly into two large bowls and add juice. Add Old-Fashioned Herb Dumplings, sprinkle with chives, and serve.

Yield: 2 servings

Seafood Bimini with Basil-Garlic Sauce

What a sight to see! A delicious combination of seafood piled on a plate of fresh pasta is gorgeous and scrumptious. The secret to serving this dish is the presentation of the plates.

Preheat oven to 325°F.

2	4-*ounce* DOLPHIN FILLETS, *boneless and skinless*
6	*large* SHRIMP, *peeled and deveined*
2	*ounces* SEA SCALLOPS
6	MUSSELS, *washed and debearded*
6	CLAMS, *washed*
8	*ounces* FETTUCCINE PASTA *(see page 146)*

Basil-Garlic Sauce

1	*tablespoon* BUTTER
2	*tablespoons* GARLIC, *minced*
¼	*cup* DRY WHITE WINE
¼	*cup* HEAVY CREAM
1	*cup* CLAM VELOUTÉ *(see page 29)*
	LEMON, *squeezed for juice*
2	*tablespoons* BASIL, *chopped*

Garnish

LEMON CROWNS, PARSLEY SPRIGS

To make Basil-Garlic Sauce, melt butter in a sauté pan over moderate heat. Add garlic and sauté for 2 to 3 minutes. Add white wine and reduce. Next add heavy cream and reduce, stirring constantly. Add velouté and simmer for 4 to 6 minutes. Add lemon juice and basil; set to the side.

Prepare seafood as listed above and lay flat in a greased shallow baking pan. Pour Basil-Garlic Sauce over seafood.

Bake seafood at 325°F for 8 to 12 minutes or until done. Cook pasta and place on two plates. Take seafood and place on top of pasta with shellfish on the side of plate and fish in the middle. Dribble with extra sauce and garnish with lemon crowns and parsley sprigs.

Yield: 2 servings

Fort Lauderdale Seafood Celebration with Béchamel Sauce

This grand "seafood celebration" is a festival of sautéed seafood placed over a halved lobster.

1	*1-pound* LOBSTER, *cooked and split in half*
4	*ounces* FISH FILLETS, *boneless and skinless*
4	*large* SHRIMP, *peeled and deveined*
¼	*pound* SEA SCALLOPS, *cleaned of muscle*
6	MUSSELS, *washed and debearded*
3	*ounces* CRABMEAT *(check for shells)*
1	*tablespoon* VEGETABLE OIL
1	*teaspoon* GARLIC, *minced*
½	GREEN PEPPER, *diced fine*
½	RED BELL PEPPER, *diced fine*
¼	RED ONION, *diced fine*
¼	*cup* SHERRY
½	LEMON, *squeezed for juice*
1	*tablespoon fresh* PARSLEY, *chopped*

Sauce

1	*cup* BÉCHAMEL SAUCE *(see page 30)*

Garnish

LEMON CROWNS, PARSLEY SPRIGS

Prepare Béchamel Sauce on the thick side. Set aside.

Cook lobster in a pot of boiling water for 7 to 8 minutes or until done. Using splitting technique on page 78, split lobster in half and clean, then place to the side. (Save the water, since it will be used later to reheat the lobster.)

In large sauté pan over moderate heat, combine oil, garlic, and vegetables. Cook vegetables for 3 to 4 minutes. Next add seafood; cook until seafood is three-quarters of the way done, about 4 to 5 minutes, stirring constantly. Add sherry and simmer 2 minutes. Add Béchamel Sauce, lemon juice, and parsley while simmering; continue to stir constantly.

Reheat lobster halves in the water that was set aside earlier or in a 250°F oven for 3 minutes. Place split side up on plate. Pour seafood mix on top of lobster halves and garnish with lemon crowns and parsley sprigs.

Yield: 2 servings

Seafood Crepes with Sherry-Paprika Sauce

The French word for thin pancakes is "crepes." Sherry is a good cooking wine and adds a nice taste to seafood. In this dish, you will be making very thin pancakes and filling with seafood mix. Fold over and smother with extra sauce, then serve.

4	ounces FISH CHUNKS, *skinless and boneless*
10	medium SHRIMP, *peeled and deveined*
8	large SEA SCALLOPS, *muscle removed*
2	ounces CRABMEAT *(check for shells)*
1	tablespoon BUTTER
1	tablespoon PAPRIKA
2	tablespoons SHALLOTS, *minced*
¼	cup DRY SHERRY
1	LEMON, *squeezed for juice*
2	tablespoons CHIVES, *chopped*
4	CREPE SHELLS *(see page 158)*

Béchamel Sauce made with heavy cream (see page 30)

Garnish

LEMON CROWNS, PARSLEY SPRIGS

Prepare seafood for cooking as indicated. In large sauté pan over moderate heat, combine butter, paprika, seafood, and shallots. Sauté until seafood is cooked, approximately 6 minutes, gently turning to keep seafood from sticking to the bottom.

Add sherry and cook until sherry is reduced by half. Next, add Béchamel Sauce, lemon juice, and chives. Blend, then lower heat and simmer 3 minutes. Remove from heat. Using two-thirds of the seafood mix, stuff crepes and place on plates. Repeat until all crepes are stuffed, two per plate. Place remaining mix on top of each crepe. Garnish with lemon crowns and parsley sprigs.

Yield: 2 servings

Seafood Medley with Creamy Tomato-Basil Sauce

In this recipe, a tasty display of seafood will be grilled to perfection, served on a bed of fresh pasta, and served with a Creamy Tomato-Basil Sauce. The grill marks on the seafood add to the beauty of the presentation.

Preheat grill.

1	4-ounce SALMON FILLET, *boneless and skinless*
1	4-ounce SNAPPER FILLET, *boneless and skinless*
4	large SHRIMP, *peeled and deveined*
8	large SEA SCALLOPS, *muscles removed*
8	ounces FETTUCCINE PASTA (*see page 146*)

Creamy Tomato-Basil Sauce

2	cups TOMATO-BASIL SAUCE (*see page 37*)
1	tablespoon OLIVE OIL
¼	cup ONION, *chopped fine*
¼	cup DRY WHITE WINE
½	cup HEAVY CREAM

Classic Herb-Citrus Marinade (see page 23)

Garnish

2	SCALLION FLOWERS (*see page 130*)
	LEMON CROWNS, PARSLEY SPRIGS

To prepare Creamy Tomato-Basil Sauce, combine onion, olive oil, and wine in a sauté pan over moderate heat. Cook until reduced by half. Add heavy cream and reduce until cream thickens. Add Tomato-Basil Sauce and simmer for 12 minutes over low heat, stirring constantly.

In mixing bowl, prepare Classic Herb-Citrus Marinade. Halve each fish fillet lengthwise. Place fish, shrimp, and scallops in marinade for 30 minutes. Cook seafood on hot grill, turning when necessary to cook each side.

While seafood is grilling, cook pasta. Drain pasta and place on two plates. Place grilled seafood neatly on other side of plate. Pour sauce over pasta. Garnish plate using Scallion Flowers, lemon crowns, and parsley sprigs.

Yield: 2 servings

"Key Biscayne" Seafood Stir Fry with Honey-Sesame Marinade

A fantastic dish to serve over rice or pasta. The recipe can be spicy or mild, depending on the amount of chili paste used. If you don't like it spicy, eliminate the paste. The secret to this recipe is to cook seafood and vegetables over high heat to seal in flavor and make vegetables crispy. Note: This recipe calls for overnight marinating.

2	tablespoons CORNSTARCH
3	ounces SWORDFISH, *cut into bite-size pieces*
6	large SHRIMP, *peeled and deveined*
4	ounces SEA SCALLOPS
1	CARROT, *julienned*
½	RED ONION, *sliced thin*
6	MUSHROOMS, *sliced*
½	head BROCCOLI, *florets only*

Honey-Sesame Marinade

3	tablespoons SOY SAUCE
3	tablespoons TERIYAKI SAUCE
¼	cup SESAME OIL
2	tablespoons VEGETABLE OIL
¼	cup PINEAPPLE JUICE
¼	cup HONEY
2	tablespoons BROWN SUGAR
1	tablespoon fresh GINGER, *minced*
1	teaspoon GARLIC, *minced*
¼	teaspoon CHILI PASTE

Yellow Saffron Rice (see page 140)

Garnish

½	cup GREEN ONIONS, *chopped*
1	tablespoon SESAME SEEDS

To prepare marinade, combine and thoroughly mix the ingredients listed for Honey-Sesame Marinade in a large mixing bowl. Place the seafood in the marinade and let sit for 24 hours.

The next day, drain seafood and save marinade (it will later be turned into a glaze). Combine cornstarch and marinade, mix well, and set to the side.

Next, preheat wok or large-size sauté pan. Add seafood and cook 2 to 3 minutes. Next add carrots, onions, mushrooms, and broccoli florets; continue cooking until seafood and vegetables are fully cooked, about 6 minutes. Add marinade to wok and stir until liquid boils and thickens. Remove from heat and serve over Yellow Saffron Rice. Garnish with green onions and sesame seeds.

Yield: 2 servings

Scallops, Calamari, and Shrimp

Since a few of these recipes use shrimp, some suggestions for preparing shrimp follow.

How to Clean and Butterfly Shrimp

Removal of the black intestine (deveining) should be done to all shrimp before you eat them. Butterflying the shrimp after it has been peeled and deveined will create a large breading surface and speed up cooking time by reducing thickness.

Using a small, sharp knife, make a shallow cut along the back side of the shrimp. To remove shells from shrimp, use your fingers to peel towards the side. (For deep-fried, broiled, and cocktail shrimp, leave the tails on for a pleasant appearance.) Lift shell up and over the meat and peel around to other side. Discard shells.

To devein shrimp, use a paring knife to make a small cut along the back side of the shrimp, then lift out the dark vein with knife tip. (You may find this easier to do under cold running water.)

To butterfly shrimp, make the existing cut on the back side of shrimp (made during deveining) a bit deeper so the shrimp can be spread open.

Recipes

Broiled Scallops with Palm Beach Herb Butter

This unique blend of ten herbs and spices will have the scallops jumping off the plate right into your mouth! Palm Beach Herb Butter can also be used on a wide variety of seafood to accentuate the flavor. For this recipe, you will need baking dishes called "boats."

Preheat oven to 325°F.

16	ounces SEA SCALLOPS, *with muscle on side removed*
½	cup DRY BREAD CRUMBS
1	teaspoon PAPRIKA, *as needed*

Palm Beach Herb Butter

6	tablespoons BUTTER *or* MARGARINE
1	tablespoon GARLIC, *minced*
¼	teaspoon GARLIC SALT
¼	cup DRY WHITE WINE
¼	teaspoon COLEMAN'S MUSTARD
⅛	teaspoon CRUSHED RED PEPPER
¼	tablespoon dry OREGANO LEAVES
¼	tablespoon dry BASIL LEAVES
¼	tablespoon dry TARRAGON LEAVES
½	LEMON, *squeezed for juice*
1	teaspoon WORCESTERSHIRE SAUCE
	SALT *and* PEPPER *to taste*

Garnish

2	SCALLION FLOWERS (*see page 130*)
	LEMON CROWNS

To make Palm Beach Herb Butter, melt butter in sauté pan over moderate heat. Remove from heat and add remaining ingredients listed for the herb butter; blend thoroughly.

Remove muscle on the side of scallops. Place equal amounts of scallops into two baking dishes (called boats). Pour Palm Beach Herb Butter over top. Sprinkle bread crumbs over scallops (it will soak up a little liquid and add flavor). Sprinkle with paprika.

Bake scallops at 325°F for 10 to 12 minutes or until done. Remove boats from oven and place on plates. Garnish with Scallion Flowers and lemon crowns and serve.

Yield: 2 servings

Cancun Coconut Shrimp with Peachy Dipping Sauce and Fried Plantains
Coconut shrimp are a favorite of mine. Try 'em; you'll like 'em too!

Set deep fryer to 350°F (or heat oil in a 2-quart heavy saucepan over medium heat and use a deep-fat thermometer to gauge temperate).

10	large SHRIMP, *peeled and deveined*
½	cup FLOUR
½	cup COCONUT, *shredded*
¼	cup UNSALTED PEANUTS

1   large EGG, *beaten*
½   *tablespoon* SOY SAUCE
1   PLANTAIN, *green*
     ICE WATER
     OIL, *for deep frying*
     SALT, *as needed*

Peachy Dipping Sauce
1   *8-ounce can sliced* PEACHES, *drained*
2   *tablespoons* BROWN SUGAR
2   *tablespoons* KETCHUP
1   *tablespoon* RICE VINEGAR
1   *tablespoon* SOY SAUCE
2   *teaspoons* CORNSTARCH

Garnish
2   SCALLION FLOWERS *(see page 130)*
     PARSLEY SPRIGS

Place coconut and peanuts in food processor and grind using an on/off pulsing action until peanuts are ground.

Toss shrimp in flour until well coated. In a small mixing bowl, combine egg, soy sauce, and salt. Add shrimp to egg mixture; toss until coated. Lightly coat with coconut-peanut mixture. Refrigerate until ready to cook.

Peel plantain and cut crosswise in half. Using a large knife, carefully slice each section lengthwise into ¼-inch thick slices. Soak in ice water for 10 minutes. Drain plantains and fry each piece in the deep fryer, with oil set at 350°F, for 2 minutes. If no deep fryer is available, a heavy 2-quart saucepan may be used instead; simply heat oil over moderate heat and use a deep-fat thermometer to gauge temperature. Remove the plantain with a long-handled spoon. Plantains should be crispy yet soft inside. Repeat until all pieces are fried. Sprinkle with salt and allow to cool to room temperature.

To prepare Peachy Dipping Sauce, combine and chop ingredients for dipping sauce in a food processor. Place mixture in a saucepan and bring to simmer over moderate heat. Boil 1 minute, or until thickened, stirring constantly. Pour into serving bowl and set aside. Sauce can be served warm or cold.

Fry sweet shrimp in deep fryer (or saucepan) at 350°F, a few pieces at a time, for 4–6 minutes or until just golden brown. Adjust heat to allow temperature to return to 350°F between each batch. Arrange on plates with garnish and serve.

Yield: 2 servings

Shrimp and Broccoli with Roasted Garlic and Red Peppers

A wonderful selection of colorful and tasty ingredients that complement each other perfectly, all served over pasta, will be a dinner treat. Roasted garlic tops it all off.

1	*large* ROASTED RED BELL PEPPER *(see page 131)*
2	*cloves* ROASTED GARLIC *(see page 131)*
¼	*cup* OLIVE OIL
10	*large* SHRIMP, *peeled and deveined*
1	*head* BROCCOLI, *florets only*
½	*cup* DRY WHITE WINE
½	LEMON, *squeezed for juice*
¼	*cup fresh* BASIL, *chopped*
8	*ounces* FETTUCCINE PASTA *(see page 146)*
1	*cup* CLAM VELOUTÉ *(see page 29)*

Garnish

2	SCALLION FLOWERS *(see page 130)*
	LEMON CROWNS

Roast peppers and cut julienne style. Set to the side.

Roast garlic. Set to the side.

Prepare Fettuccine Pasta and set to the side.

In preheated sauté pan over moderate heat, combine olive oil, shrimp, and broccoli. Cook for 2 to 3 minutes, stirring constantly. Add white wine and simmer 1 minute. Add roasted pepper, roasted garlic, Clam Velouté, lemon juice, and basil; simmer for 3 to 4 minutes, stirring to cook broccoli on all sides. Remove seafood from heat and serve over Fettucine Pasta. Garnish with Scallion Flowers and lemon crowns.

Yield: 2 servings

Calamari A1A with Tomato-Basil Sauce

A1A is a historic highway that runs the entire east coast of Florida.

1	*pound* SQUID *(calamari), cleaned and cut into rings (or prepared calamari, available at fish markets and grocery stores)*

1	*cup* BUTTERMILK
1	*cup all-purpose* FLOUR
1	*pinch* SALT
⅛	*teaspoon* WHITE PEPPER
¼	*cup* OLIVE OIL
2	*cups* TOMATO-BASIL SAUCE *(see page 37)*
8	*ounces* FETTUCCINE PASTA *(see page 146)*
¼	*cup fresh* BASIL, *chopped*

Garnish

LEMON CROWNS, PARSLEY SPRIGS

Prepare Tomato-Basil Sauce. Set to the side.

Cook Fettuccine Pasta. Drain and set to the side.

To clean calamari, first rinse in cold water. Pull the mantle and the tentacles apart. Cut off tentacles above the eyes, then remove the eyes and the ink sac; intestines will come away from the tentacles. On the thick part of the tentacles, squeeze; this will push the hard beak out. Discard beak. The tentacles can be left whole. On the mantle, squeeze the entrails from the body by running your fingers from the closed to the cut end. A transparent quill that protrudes from the body will appear; discard. Pull as much of the skin as possible away from the mantle. Discard the skin. Soak cleaned calamari in buttermilk for one hour.

> Cooking time should always be short for calamari!

Heat oil in sauté pan over moderate heat. Coat calamari with flour, salt, and pepper and sauté in hot oil until light golden brown, about 3 to 4 minutes, turning constantly. Add Tomato-Basil Sauce and cook until hot. Remove calamari from heat. Place equal amounts of pasta and calamari onto two plates. Sprinkle with fresh basil, garnish with lemon crowns and parsley sprigs, and serve.

Yield: 2 servings

Gallery Shrimp with Crabmeat Stuffing

In this recipe, you will butterfly large shrimp, top with a "football" made of a fantastic crabmeat mixture, and bake to perfection. This dish is impressive and easy to prepare!

Preheat oven to 325°F.

10	*large* SHRIMP, *peeled, deveined, and butterflied, with tails left on*

¼ *cup* DRY WHITE WINE

¼ *cup* WATER

⅛ *cup* MELTED BUTTER

PAPRIKA, *for color*

Crabmeat Stuffing

4 *ounces* CRABMEAT (*check for bits of shell*)

4 *tablespoons* BUTTER, *unsalted*

1 *tablespoon* GARLIC, *minced*

¼ *cup* ONION, *chopped fine*

¼ *cup* CELERY, *chopped fine*

¼ *cup* DRY WHITE WINE

1 *teaspoon* WORCESTERSHIRE SAUCE

¼ *teaspoon* TABASCO SAUCE

1 *medium* EGG

4 *cups* WHITE BREAD CRUMBS, *fresh*

Yellow Saffron Rice (see page 140)

Garnish

LEMON CROWNS, PARSLEY SPRIGS

To make Crabmeat Stuffing, in sauté pan over moderate heat, melt butter and add garlic, onion, and celery. Cook until celery is tender, about 10 minutes. Add white wine, Worcestershire, and Tabasco; simmer for 3 to 4 minutes. Place mixture in bowl and add crabmeat, egg, and bread crumbs. Mix thoroughly. Let mix cool, then form 10 equal balls.

Place butterflied shrimp in baking pan, insides down. Place a ball of stuffing on each shrimp and form to shrimp by gently pressing down. Turn tail up towards stuffing. Sprinkle top with paprika. Add white wine, butter, and water to pan. Bake at 325°F for 8 to 10 minutes or until stuffing has a light brown color and is hot inside.

Remove shrimp from oven and serve on bed of Yellow Saffron Rice. Garnish with lemon crowns and parsley sprigs and serve.

Yield: 2 servings

Shrimp and Scallops with Fra Diavolo Sauce

This recipe is a treasure lost and found—for years, many cooks simply added crushed red pepper to tomato sauce in order to make Fra Diavolo. Now you will learn the secret way to prepare the "devilish"

combination of sauces to create this dish. Note: This recipe calls for a wide range of fresh ingredients.

8   large SHRIMP, *peeled and deveined*
8   large SEA SCALLOPS, *muscles removed*
1   *tablespoon* OLIVE OIL

Fra Diavolo Sauce
1   *cup* FENNEL TOMATO-BASIL SAUCE *(see pages 31)*
¼   *cup (per serving)* PANCETTA BACON BUTTER *(see pages 31)*
     FETTUCCINE PASTA *(see page 146)*

Garnish
     LEMON CROWNS, PARSLEY SPRIGS

You will prepare two sauces; one is Fennel Tomato-Basil and the other is Pancetta Bacon Butter. Set the sauces to the side and do not mix them together.

Next, prepare Fettuccine Pasta. Set to the side.

In large sauté pan over moderate heat, combine olive oil, shrimp, and scallops; cook for 2 minutes on each side. Add seasoned Fennel Tomato-Basil Sauce and simmer for 3 to 4 minutes until hot. At the last minute, directly before serving, whisk in Pancetta Bacon Butter until completely melted; remove from heat. Serve the shrimp and scallops on top of the pasta and smother with excess sauce. Garnish with lemon crowns and parsley sprigs.

Yield: 2 servings

Pizza

Pizza tastes great topped with seafood. Try the recipes below and get creative—add some of your own favorite ingredients and seasonings.

Grilled, Hand-Formed Cornmeal Pizza Dough

Rich pizza dough is made with oil. This dough is simple to prepare and ready to use in about 1 hour. Pizza dough can be prepared entirely by hand or started in a food processor.

Preheat grill.

1½	teaspoons	ACTIVE DRY YEAST
¾	cup	WARM WATER, *about 105°F*
2	tablespoons	OLIVE OIL
1½	cups	UNBLEACHED FLOUR *or* BREAD FLOUR
1	cup	CORNMEAL
1	teaspoon	SALT

Dissolve yeast in warm water in small bowl and let sit 5 minutes. Mix in olive oil. In a large bowl, combine flour, cornmeal, and salt. Add yeast mixture and stir until dough just barely holds together.

Place dough on a lightly floured surface and knead until soft, adding a little more flour if necessary. Put dough in an oiled bowl and turn to coat dough with oil. Cover bowl with plastic and let dough rise in a warm place until it doubles in size, about 1 hour. Use dough for any pizza recipe. Pizza dough can be frozen or refrigerated for up to one week. (Wrap airtight and thaw in refrigerator for one day if frozen.)

Lay out dough on well-floured cutting board and cut in half. Using floured hands, flatten out dough and shape. Make pizza dough about ½- to ⅓-inch thick.

Preheat grill. Oil the grill well to keep the dough from sticking. Grill on each side for 2 to 3 minutes. Keep fire low so dough does not burn.

When done, remove and set aside, or refrigerate for later use.

Yield: 2 pizzas

Grilled Cornmeal Pizza with Bay Scallops and Mornay Sauce

Cornmeal pizzas are easy and fun to create. In this recipe, you will combine a white sauce and fresh ingredients for a delicious pizza.

Preheat oven to 350°F.

 2 CORNMEAL PIZZAS, *formed and grilled (see page 126)*
 6 *ounces* BAY SCALLOPS, *drained*
 4 MUSHROOMS, *sliced thin*
 ¼ *cup* FRESH BASIL, *chopped*
 1 *cup* MORNAY SAUCE *(see page 30)*

Place mushrooms in small pan of hot water and let sit 2 minutes. Drain thoroughly.

Pizza also makes a great appetizer to start your party!

Lay out grilled pizza dough and spread Mornay Sauce on top. Place bay scallops and mushrooms in a neat fashion on pizzas.

Bake pizzas at 350°F until well browned and puffy, about 10 to 12 minutes. If available, use a pizza oven or a baking stone to cook pizza. If not available, cooking pizza on a cookie sheet in a regular oven will work.

Sprinkle pizzas with freshly chopped basil right before serving. Cut pizzas and serve hot.

Yield: 2 servings

Grilled Cornmeal Pizza with Shrimp and Roasted Peppers

While preparing pizzas, add your own special ingredients to satisfy your own creative taste!

Preheat oven to 350°F.

 2 CORNMEAL PIZZA CRUSTS, *formed and grilled (see page 126)*
 2 ROASTED GREEN *and* YELLOW BELL PEPPERS, *one of each (see page 131)*
 8 *ounces* BABY SHRIMP, *peeled and deveined*
 4 *ounces* MOZZARELLA CHEESE, *shredded*
 4 *canned* ARTICHOKE HEARTS, *cut in half*
 ¼ *cup fresh* BASIL, *chopped*

Tomato-Basil Sauce (see page 37)

Pizza might be a simple dish, but always use the best ingredients.

Prepare Tomato-Basil Sauce. Set to the side.

Roast peppers, peel, and slice into thin strips. Set aside.

Lay out grilled pizza dough and spread with Tomato-Basil Sauce. Cover pizza with shredded Mozzarella cheese, shrimp, peppers, and artichokes. Bake at 350°F until well browned and puffy, about 10 to 12 minutes. If available, use a pizza oven or a baking stone to cook pizza. Cooking pizzas on a cookie sheet in a regular oven will do as an alternative.

Sprinkle pizzas with freshly chopped basil right before serving. Cut pizzas and serve hot.

Yield: 2 servings

RECIPES
Meal Accompaniments

Vegetables, Potatoes, and Rice

Vegetable Tips

You should give as much attention to preparing your vegetables as you give to preparing the meat. A well-seasoned vegetable is both a pleasure to eat and very nutritious.

Modern methods of preparation and shipping make almost every vegetable available at your market, in any season. There is no excuse for monotony in your vegetable diet.

The most important rule about cooking vegetables is to avoid over-cooking. Properly cooked vegetables should never be limp or soggy but have a bit of crunch to them. Steaming vegetables is advantageous in keeping the nutrients in the vegetables and the colors bright. The following are the benefits of properly cooked vegetables:

Retaining nutritional value: Cook vegetables for as short a time as possible. Steaming vegetables will help avoid loss of nutrients. Baking vegetables in their skin will prevent loss of water-soluble nutrients. Potatoes and winter squash are prepared this way.

Retaining natural color: A short cooking time is also of great advantage here. Cooking processes reduce the chlorophyll content of green vegetables. For white and red vegetables, a small amount of vinegar or lemon juice added to the water will help prevent color changes.

Obtaining excellent flavor: The freshness of vegetables will directly affect their flavor when cooked. As vegetables lose their freshness, some of the sugar turns to starch, and they lose some sweetness. In addition, some of the flavor compounds of vegetables will escape during cooking.

Keeping a pleasing texture: Vegetables should have desirable texture (slightly crisp) and should not be mushy when cooked. As always, opinions will vary with respect to what is considered desirable texture for cooked vegetables.

Julienne-style Cutting

Julienne-style cutting is the cutting of vegetables or fruit in strips, approximately ¼-inch x ¼-inch x 2½–3 inches in size. Cutting food products into uniform shapes and sizes ensures even cooking and enhances appearance. Cut vegetables such as carrots and rutabagas into ¼-inch thick slices, then cut into ¼-inch strips. Vegetables such as peppers and leeks can be cut in half, then laid flat and cut into strips.

Cutting Scallion Flowers

Scallions are white onions that are harvested when young. Scallions are primarily used as edible garnish, despite their strong flavor. Choose scallions with well-developed bulbs for preparing flowers. Use a bulb with a three-inch length of stalk. With a paring knife, make many thin slits into thick end. Only cut halfway through. Allow the flower to open in ice water. Use for garnishing seafood.

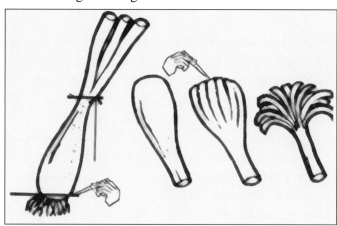

Roasting and Peeling Peppers

Hold or place 1 to 2 peppers over open gas flame or charcoal fire, or place under broiler. Turn often to blacken all sides. When blackened, place in a bowl and cover tightly with plastic wrap. Set to the side until cool, about 15 to 20 minutes.

Peel peppers, cut them in half, and remove the stem and seeds. Lay halves flat and, using the dull side of a knife, scrape away any black bits of skin and stray seeds. Cut into strips.

Tomato Concassé

Tomato concassé is made with peeled, deseeded, chopped tomatoes. The word "concassé" literally means to chop coarsely.

Use 2 to 3 large vine-ripe tomatoes. Remove core of tomato and cut an X on the bottom using a sharp knife. Plunge tomato into a saucepan of boiling water and cook until skin begins to peel away, approximately 30 to 50 seconds.

Remove from saucepan and let cool. Peel off skins. Cut tomatoes in half and remove seeds (if necessary, run under cold water to wash out seeds). They are now ready to be diced or cut into strips.

Yield: 1½+ cups

Roasting Garlic

Method One: Using a knife, slice 1 to 3 whole garlic bulbs in half, dribble with olive oil, wrap in tin foil, and place in preheated 350°F oven. Bake for 20 minutes or until lightly brown. (Check after 20 minutes. If not done, cook longer.)

Method Two: Heat olive oil in sauté pan over moderate high heat. Sauté peeled garlic cloves until garlic starts to roast and turn light golden brown. Turn garlic over as it cooks. Garlic should be crispy on the outside and soft in the middle.

Yield: ⅛+ cup

Artichokes with Lemon Mayonnaise

Artichokes are immature flower heads of a thistlelike plant and are characterized by overlapping outer leaves.

2   medium ARTICHOKES, *fresh*
2   tablespoons SALT
1   LEMON, *squeezed for juice*

½   *cup* MAYONNAISE
18   *inches butcher string*
4   LEMON *slices*
4   LEMON *wedges*

To make Lemon Mayonnaise, combine 2 tablespoons of lemon juice and mayonnaise and blend thoroughly. Put in the refrigerator for later use.

Using kitchen scissors and knife, trim the spiny tips off the leaves of the artichokes. Using butcher string, tie lemon slices on top and bottom of artichokes to prevent browning. Bring water to boil in large saucepan over moderate-high heat. Add salt and artichokes; cook 30 to 40 minutes or until done. Remove artichokes from water and drain. Serve with Lemon Mayonnaise on the side. Garnish with lemon wedges.

Yield: 2 servings

Lemon-Herb Broccoli

Quick and easy! Herbs and lemon add flavor.

1   *head* BROCCOLI, *cut into florets*
½   ONION, *sliced thin*
2   *tablespoons* BUTTER *or* MARGARINE
1   LEMON, *squeezed for juice*
1   *tablespoon* DIJON MUSTARD
¾   *teaspoon dried* MARJORAM LEAVES
     SALT *and* PEPPER *to taste*

Cook broccoli and onion by steaming, or in boiling salted water until tender, yet still crispy. Melt margarine in sauté pan over moderate heat and add lemon juice, mustard, marjoram, and salt and pepper to taste. Spoon over broccoli.

Yield: 2 servings

Green Beans Almondine

This is a classic recipe and a favorite of mine. If you don't like almonds, try pecans as an alternative.

8   *ounces* WHOLE GREEN BEANS, *fresh*
1   *tablespoon* SALT
2   *tablespoons* BUTTER *or* MARGARINE

½ *tablespoon* GARLIC, *minced*
⅓ *cup sliced* ALMONDS

Snip the tips of the green beans. Bring water to a boil in saucepan over moderate heat and add salt and green beans. Cook for 9 minutes, or until tender. Drain beans thoroughly and set aside.

Combine butter, garlic, and almonds in a sauté pan over moderate heat. Sauté for 1 to 2 minutes. Add green beans and toss gently, bringing beans up to temperature before serving.

Yield: 2 servings

Asparagus Bundles

Place two of these vegetable bundles on plates when creating entrées.

¼ *pound fresh* ASPARAGUS
1 *large* CARROT, *peeled*
¼ *cup* OLIVE OIL
1-2 *cloves* GARLIC
1 *tablespoon dried* TARRAGON LEAVES
   SALT *and* WHITE PEPPER *to taste*

To prepare asparagus, cut off tough end of spears, leaving stems 3–4 inches long. You can also peel the stems with a vegetable peeler.

Wash asparagus, rinse, and place in steamer basket. Place steamer basket in large saucepan; add 1 inch of water. Cover and bring to a boil over moderately high heat; steam asparagus about 5 minutes, or until crisp and tender. Remove and set to the side.

Peel the carrot to make four long, thin slices (about 4 to 5 inches long). Steam carrot peels until slightly curled and tender.

Divide asparagus into four clusters. Wrap each cluster with a carrot slice to create a bundle. Place bundles in steamer. Cover and bring to a boil over high heat. Steam for 3 to 4 minutes or until asparagus is hot.

In a sauté pan over moderate heat, combine olive oil, garlic, and tarragon. Cook and stir until garlic is soft but not brown. Place bundles on warm serving plates and top with garlic mixture.

Season with salt and pepper and serve.

Yield: 2 servings

Parmesan Tomatoes with Asparagus Spears
Easy to make and looks great!

Preheat oven to 350°F.

1	medium ripe TOMATO, *cored and cut in half*
⅓	cup PARMESAN CHEESE, *grated*
12	ASPARAGUS *spears*
4	RED PIMENTOS, *cut into strips*
	SALT *for cooking*

Cover cut halves of tomatoes with Parmesan cheese and bake at 350°F until the Parmesan starts to brown. Set aside and keep warm.

In a saucepan over moderate heat, bring water and salt to a simmer. Add asparagus spears and cook for 4–6 minutes. Remove from water and drain. Place tomatoes on one side of plate and place 3 asparagus spears on each side in a fan shape. Place red pimentos on asparagus. Place entrée on other side of plate for a full-plate presentation.

Yield: 2 servings

Baked Squash Medley
For this recipe, use a small, but tall, baking dish.

Preheat oven to 325°F.

1	YELLOW SQUASH, *diced*
1	ZUCCHINI, *diced*
¼	cup ONION, *chopped*
½	cup CRACKER MEAL *or* BREAD CRUMBS
1	EGG, *slightly beaten*
½	cup MELTED BUTTER
¼	tablespoon GRANULATED SUGAR
	SALT *and* PEPPER *to taste*

Wash and dice squash. Boil until tender, drain thoroughly, and mash. Add onions, cracker meal, egg, 2 tablespoons of the butter, and sugar. Mix thoroughly. Add salt and pepper to taste.

Pour mixture into small baking dish and spread remaining melted butter over top. Sprinkle with bread crumbs. Bake at 325°F for 1 hour or until top is brown.

Yield: 2 servings

Grilled Vegetable Kabobs

You can use either metal or wooden skewers.

Preheat grill.

Experiment with
your favorite
vegetables.

6	*medium* MUSHROOMS
1	ZUCCHINI, *cut into 1-inch slices*
2	CHERRY TOMATOES

Classic Herb-Citrus Marinade (see page 23)

Prepare Classic Herb-Citrus Marinade. Set to the side.

Place mushrooms in medium-size bowl; cover with boiling water. Let stand 1 minute; drain. In mixing bowl, marinate vegetables in Classic Herb-Citrus Marinade.

Using two skewers, thread mushrooms and zucchini, alternating them. Grill kabobs over medium-hot coals, about 10 minutes, turning and brushing frequently with dressing mixture. Remove from heat. Thread cherry tomatoes onto ends of skewers. Continue grilling 5 minutes, turning and brushing with remaining dressing mixture.

Yield: 2 servings

Sweet Pepper–Corn Pudding

A great side dish for dinners in which a touch of sweetness is needed.

Preheat oven to 325°F.

½	*cup canned* CORN NIBLETS
1	*cup* CREAM-STYLE CORN, *canned*
½	*cup* RED *and* GREEN BELL PEPPERS, *chopped fine*
2	EGGS, *slightly beaten*
1	*tablespoon* GRANULATED SUGAR
½	*tablespoon* ARROWROOT
1	*tablespoon* RED ONION, *minced*
¼	*teaspoon* SALT
¼	*teaspoon* DRY MUSTARD
1	*tablespoon* MELTED BUTTER
	dash of SALT *and* RED *and* BLACK PEPPER
¼	*cup* MILK

Drain corn niblets; combine with eggs, creamed corn, and peppers. In a separate bowl, combine sugar, arrowroot, and seasonings. Stir into corn mixture. Add remaining ingredients, mixing well. Pour into a buttered casserole and bake at 325°F for 1 hour, stirring after 30 minutes.

Yield: 2 servings

Potato Pointers

All-purpose Idaho and Russet potatoes are best for baking. Small (white, red, or new) potatoes are best for boiling and roasting.

Baked potatoes can be served with butter or special toppings such as cheese, broccoli, shrimp, peppers, onions, bacon bits, etc. You get the idea. Mashed potatoes can also be a treat when seasoned with peas, carrots, tomatoes, or herbs. Use your imagination.

Garlic-Roasted Red Bliss Potatoes

An excellent way to serve red bliss potatoes.

Preheat oven to 325°F.

¼	*pound*	RED BLISS POTATOES
½	*cup*	CORN OIL
2	*tablespoons*	GARLIC, *minced*
2	*tablespoons*	DRY BREAD CRUMBS
1	*tablespoon*	PAPRIKA
		SALT *and* WHITE PEPPER *to taste*
		fresh PARSLEY, *chopped, as garnish (optional)*

Scrub and wash potatoes; cut in half. In large mixing bowl, combine oil, garlic, bread crumbs, paprika, salt, and pepper. Add potatoes and coat thoroughly. Place potatoes in roasting pan and bake at 325°F for 40 minutes (stirring occasionally) or until potatoes are tender and golden brown. Garnish with chopped fresh parsley, if desired.

Yield: 2 servings

Potato Wedges with Cuban White Barbecue Sauce

The corn syrup used in this barbecue sauce will make a sweet glaze. Bread crumbs add texture as well as flavor.

Preheat oven to 350°F.

3	*medium*	IDAHO POTATOES

Cuban White Barbecue Sauce
- ¼ *cup* LIQUID MARGARINE
- ¼ *cup* CORN SYRUP
- 2 *tablespoons* GARLIC, *minced*
- ⅛ *medium* ONION
- 1 *tablespoon dry* BASIL
- ⅓ *cup* DRY BREAD CRUMBS
- 1 *tablespoon* RICE VINEGAR
- 1 *teaspoon* DIJON MUSTARD
- SALT *and* WHITE PEPPER *to taste*

Scrub potatoes under running water and rinse. Dry well. Line a baking sheet with aluminum foil and spray with cooking spray.

Cut potatoes in half lengthwise, then cut each lengthwise half into 3 wedges. Place potatoes in mixing bowl and set aside.

To prepare Cuban White Barbecue Sauce, thoroughly blend margarine, syrup, garlic, onion, basil, rice vinegar, Dijon mustard, salt, and pepper in a blender of food processor. Combine Cuban White Barbecue Sauce and bread crumbs in mixing bowl with potatoes. Thoroughly coat potatoes with barbecue sauce mixture.

Place potatoes skin side down on prepared baking sheet, layering the potatoes as more are added. Bake at 350°F 25 to 40 minutes or until browned and fork-tender. Dribble with extra sauce and garnish as desired.

Yield: 2 servings

Sweet Planks with a Cinnamon Glaze

These fried wedges taste like candied yams.

Heat oil in heavy 2-quart saucepan over medium heat until fat thermometer reaches 350°F.

- 2 *medium* SWEET POTATOES
- 3 *tablespoons* SALTED BUTTER
- ¼ *cup* GRANULATED SUGAR
- 2 *tablespoons* CINNAMON, *ground*
- OIL *for deep-fat frying*

Peel sweet potatoes and cut in half lengthwise. Next, cut each half into 3 or 4 wedges, cutting at an inward angle to make planks. Par cook sweet planks in a steamer or pot of boiling water until planks are fork-tender, yet firm. Drain on paper towel.

In preheated 2-quart saucepan with fat at 350°F, deep-fry sweet planks a few pieces at a time, 4–8 minutes each time or until just golden brown. Adjust heat to allow temperature to return to 350°F between each batch.

In the meantime, stir together sugar and cinnamon in a small bowl. Heat a large sauté pan over moderate heat until super-hot (pan must be really hot to melt the sugar) and add butter, which should turn brown at once. Immediately place the fried potato planks in the hot skillet and sprinkle with cinnamon mixture. Glaze planks on all sides. Serve immediately.

Yield: 2 servings

Sweet Potato Pancakes with Cilantro Sour Cream

We have all had potato pancakes before, so in this recipe we use sweet potatoes to add a twist.

2	cups SWEET POTATOES, *peeled and grated*	
2	tablespoons SALT	
2	EGGS, *lightly beaten*	
½	cup all-purpose FLOUR	
½	teaspoon SALT	
1	tablespoon LEMON JUICE	
½	cup RED ONION, *chopped fine*	
1	tablespoon PARSLEY, *chopped*	
1	tablespoon CHIVES, *chopped*	
1	teaspoon GARLIC, *minced*	
⅛	teaspoon BLACK PEPPER	
	BUTTER, *for frying*	
½	cup SOUR CREAM	
2	tablespoons fresh CILANTRO, *chopped*	

Grate potatoes and toss with 2 tablespoons of salt. Place in colander and let stand for 30 minutes. Rinse potatoes and drain well, then pat dry with a clean kitchen towel.

In a large bowl, combine sweet potatoes, eggs, flour, ½ teaspoon salt, lemon juice, red onion, parsley, chives, garlic, and pepper. Mix thoroughly and let stand for 20 minutes.

In a sauté pan over moderate heat, melt enough butter to coat bottom of pan. Drop tablespoon-size amounts of batter into pan and fry on both sides until brown. Remove the potato pancakes from pan and drain grease on paper towel. Garnish with sour cream and fresh cilantro. Serve immediately.

Yield: 2 servings

Rice Review

The way in which rice is cooked depends on both the type of rice and the particular recipe.

Rice can be used in many recipes and served at various times of the day; breakfast cereals, desserts, and side dishes often use rice. Rice can also be served as a starchy replacement for potatoes.

The first rule to follow when cooking rice is to read the instructions on the package. Different rice requires different amounts of water and different cooking times.

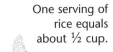

One serving of rice equals about ½ cup.

Rice Yield

‣1 cup of uncooked white rice will yield 3 cups of cooked rice

‣1 cup of uncooked converted, parboiled, or brown rice will yield 4 cups of cooked rice

‣1 cup of instant, precooked rice will yield 2 cups of cooked rice

Types of Rice

Rice grows in three grains, or lengths: short, medium, and long. The difference between white and brown rice is caused by different milling processes after harvest.

Some types of rice sold in the supermarkets include:

Short-Grained: arborio rice, brown rice, enriched white rice, and precooked (instant) rice

Long-Grained: brown rice, converted rice, enriched white rice, precooked (instant) rice, and wild rice

Serving Rice

The easiest way to prepare rice is to cook it, season it, and spoon it into a serving dish. Rice can also be served in more elegant ways.

A molded ring of rice can be served by itself or with a filling. Rice can be also be compressed into almost any shape (in a well-greased container), which it will keep when served. Molded rice always adds a festive touch to any meal.

Seasoned Rice

Rice can be cooked with bouillon cubes for flavor. If you want plain rice, omit bouillon and add 1 teaspoon salt.

1	*cup*	LONG-GRAIN RICE
2½	*cups*	WATER
½	*tablespoon*	BUTTER
1		BOUILLON CUBE, *chicken base*

Combine water and bouillon cube in a medium saucepan. Bring to a boil over moderate heat. Add rice and butter. Cover and simmer about 20 minutes, or until most of the liquid has been absorbed. Remove from heat. Let stand for 5 minutes. Fluff with a fork and serve.

Yield: 3–4 cups

Yellow Saffron Rice

Saffron is a yellow-orange stigma from a small purple crocus and is the world's most expensive spice. A little saffron goes a long way and is used to flavor, as well as tint, food. Saffron comes in threads and powdered form.

1	*cup*	LONG-GRAIN RICE
2	*tablespoons*	BUTTER
¼		ONION, *chopped*
¼	*teaspoon fresh*	SAFFRON, *chopped fine*
2	*cups*	CHICKEN CONSOMMÉ
⅛	*teaspoon*	WHITE PEPPER
¼		RED BELL PEPPER, *chopped*

Chop onion and saffron together on a cutting board; this will help extract flavor and color from the saffron threads. Place onion and saffron in medium saucepan over moderate heat, scraping the cutting board for any excess saffron. Add butter and cook about 4 to 5 minutes until onion is transparent. Add chicken consommé, rice, and white and red pepper. Mix thoroughly. Lower heat and simmer for 20 minutes, stirring 3 to 4 times while cooking. Test rice for tenderness; cook a little longer if needed. Serve immediately.

Yield: 2 servings

Caribbean Black Beans and Rice

This is a favorite side dish of mine that can also be a complete meal in itself.

Note: The beans will need to be soaked overnight.

½	*pound* DRIED BLACK BEANS
3	*cups* WATER
1	*tablespoon* OLIVE OIL
1	*medium* ONION, *chopped*
2	*tablespoons* GARLIC, *minced*
1	BAY LEAF
¼	*teaspoon* CUMIN
⅛	*teaspoon dry* OREGANO
½	*teaspoon* SALT
1	*tablespoon* DRY SHERRY
1	*tablespoon* APPLE CIDER VINEGAR
½	*tablespoon* TABASCO SAUCE
1	*teaspoon* SUGAR
2	*cups* COOKED WHITE RICE, *still hot*
¼	*cup* ONION, *chopped for garnish*
	HOT SAUCE

Discard any shriveled beans, then place in colander and wash several times. Place beans in a large pan and cover with water. Soak overnight.

After soaking for 24 hours, drain the beans and rinse them in fresh water. Combine clean, soaked beans with 3 cups of fresh water in sauce pot. Bring to a boil over high heat. Reduce heat to a simmer. Cook for 45 minutes.

In a separate sauté pan, combine olive oil and garlic; cook 1 minute. Add chopped onion and bay leaf and sauté over moderate heat for 20 minutes. Add onion mixture to beans, then add cumin, oregano, salt, Tabasco, sherry, vinegar, and sugar. Simmer another 30 to 40 minutes until beans are tender but not mushy. Add more water during the course of boiling if there is not enough to keep the beans covered. Remove bay leaf.

Serve beans on top of prepared rice. Sprinkle with chopped onions and serve. Serve with hot sauce on the side.

Yield: 4 servings

Old-Fashioned Herb Dumplings

Dumplings are easy to make. Savory dumplings are prepared by placing small mounds of dough in soup and cooking them until done. Precooked dumplings can also be added to stew or soup.

Preheat oven to 325°F.

1½	cups MILK
1	ounce BUTTER
½	teaspoon SALT
¼	cup SEMOLINA FLOUR
1	EGG YOLK, *beaten*
⅓	cup PARMESAN CHEESE, *grated*
2	teaspoons PARSLEY, *chopped*
2	teaspoons CHIVES, *chopped*

In ovenproof saucepan, combine milk, butter, and salt and bring the mixture to a boil over moderate heat. Add semolina and herbs a little at a time, stirring constantly with a whisk to avoid lumps. Bring mixture to a boil. Remove from heat, cover, and bake at 325°F for 7 to 8 minutes. Remove from oven.

Add egg yolks and Parmesan cheese and mix thoroughly. Spread out mixture on small sheet pan until ¼-inch thick and cool.

Cut dumplings into ½ x ¼–inch rectangle squares and set to the side. When you are ready to serve the meal, drop the squares into boiling water for 20 to 30 seconds. Drain, then serve immediately with your favorite dish.

Yield: 2 servings

Bread and Pasta

How to Knead

Kneading means to repeatedly fold over and press together dough, usually by hand. Kneading smooths dough and develops the gluten that gives it the elasticity to hold together as it expands.

To knead dough, gently pick up dough from the side that faces away from you. Fold over toward you. Press out lightly with palm of hand. Give the dough a quarter turn. Repeat ten times. Gently roll out dough from center to ¾-inch thickness.

Homemade Garlic Croutons

Preheat oven to 325°F.

4	*slices* WHITE BREAD
2	*tablespoons* OLIVE OIL
1	*teaspoon* GARLIC, *minced*
½	*teaspoon dry* BASIL

Take 4 slices of white bread and cut into bite-size squares. Lay out on baking pan. In mixing bowl, blend olive oil, garlic, and basil. Dribble mixture on top of croutons while turning and tossing gently so croutons are seasoned on all sides. Bake at 325°F for 5 to 10 minutes or until croutons are dry and crispy, with a light golden color.

Old-Fashioned Buttermilk Biscuits

Biscuits always have a homemade flavor and a taste that goes great with seafood dishes!

Preheat oven to 400°F.

2	*cups all-purpose* FLOUR, *sifted*
2¼	*teaspoons* BAKING POWDER
1	*teaspoon* SALT
⅓	*cup* SHORTENING, *room temperature*
¾	*cup* BUTTERMILK

MELTED BUTTER

PARMESAN CHEESE, *grated*

Honey Butter

2   *tablespoons* HONEY

8   *ounces* LIGHTLY SALTED BUTTER

Sift together flour, baking powder, and salt into medium bowl. Cut shortening into flour mixture using a pastry blender (or two knives in scissor motion) until mixture resembles coarse cornmeal. Make a well in the center and pour in buttermilk all at once, then stir quickly with a fork. If mixture seems dry, add more buttermilk. Dough should be moist enough to be able to be formed into a ball (mix should not be too wet, or it will stick to sides of bowl). Place dough onto lightly floured surface to knead.

Make six balls out of the dough and place on ungreased cookie sheet. Coat top with melted butter. Bake at 400°F for 12 to 14 minutes. Remove from oven, sprinkle each ball with Parmesan cheese, and place back in oven for 5 more minutes or until biscuits are fully cooked inside. Mix honey with butter and serve with biscuits.

Yield: 6 biscuits

Onion-and-Herb Flat Bread

This bread is easy to make; it's a simple yeast dough that is flattened and baked. Serve with soup, salad, and entrée, and your guests will be delighted.

Preheat oven to 400°F.

1¼   *cups* WARM WATER

¾   *teaspoon* SUGAR

1   *package* ACTIVE DRY YEAST

2¾   *cups* UNBLEACHED FLOUR

3   *tablespoons* UNSALTED BUTTER

½   *cup* ONION, *chopped*

½   *cup fresh* BASIL, *chopped*

½   *teaspoon* COARSE SEA SALT

¼   *teaspoon ground* BLACK PEPPER

¼   *cup* OLIVE OIL

½   *cup* CORNMEAL

Combine ½ cup warm water, sugar, and yeast; let sit for 10 minutes until yeast softens. Mix in 1 cup flour and stir thoroughly. Cover and let mix rise for 2 to 3 hours.

While dough is rising, combine butter and onions in a sauté pan and cook over medium heat until soft, about 6 to 8 minutes. Remove onion from heat and combine with basil, coarse salt, and pepper. Set to the side.

Mix remaining 2 cups of flour, 2 tablespoons olive oil, and ½ cup water to dough mix. Blend thoroughly. On a lightly floured surface, knead dough (following the directions on page 143). Lightly coat dough with extra olive oil on all sides and place in bowl. Cover and let rise 90 minutes.

Punch down dough into a flat, 8 x 8 inch square shape. Sprinkle a pan with cornmeal; place dough on it. Spread onion mix evenly on top of dough, using extra olive oil to lightly dribble on top. Bake in 400°F oven for 17 to 24 minutes or until golden brown.

Yield: 4 servings

Hush Puppies

What would a fish fry be without hush puppies?

Heat oil to 350°F.

1	*cup* CORNMEAL	
1½	*tablespoons* BAKING POWDER	
2	*tablespoons* GRANULATED SUGAR	
½	*teaspoon* SALT	
⅛	*teaspoon* CRUSHED RED PEPPER	
2	*tablespoons* ONIONS, *chopped fine*	
1	*large* EGG	
¼	*cup* MILK	
½	*tablespoon* PARSLEY, *chopped*	

Lemon Cocktail Sauce (see page 25)

Garnish

    LEMON WEDGES

Mix all dry ingredients in bowl. Add onion, egg, milk, and parsley; blend well. Refrigerate until ready to use. Spoon into deep fat heated to

350°F and fry 2 to 4 minutes or until golden brown. Adjust heat in between batches to maintain temperature at 350°F. Serve with Lemon Cocktail Sauce and lemon wedges.

Yield: 1 dozen

Fresh Pasta Dough

Since fresh pasta is made from eggs, the dough must be used within a couple of days. Fresh pasta cooks in a fraction of the time required for dry pasta. Listed below is a basic recipe, followed by a few simple variations.

2	*cups* SEMOLINA *or* ALL-PURPOSE FLOUR
⅓	*cup plus 2 teaspoons* WATER
2	EGGS, *at room temperature*
2	*teaspoons* VEGETABLE OIL
½	*teaspoon* SALT

Combine flour, water, eggs, oil, and salt in a large bowl. Knead mixture to a smooth paste (see page 143 for kneading technique). Cover the dough and let sit for 45 minutes.

After dough has rested, dust work area with flour. Remove dough from mixing bowl and place on dusted surface. Flatten out dough with a rolling pin, flipping dough over occasionally while rolling and frequently dusting work surface. Continue rolling dough until it is about ⅛-inch thick. Place the sheet of dough on a clean surface to dry. After drying, cut into strips, or the shape desired, with a sharp knife or pasta cutter.

Variations: For basil pasta dough, add 1 tablespoon of dry basil leaves to above recipe. For black peppercorn pasta dough, add 1 tablespoon of cracked black peppercorns.

Yield: 2 servings

Shaping Pasta Dough

There is a wide array of pasta-forming equipment available at specialty gourmet shops and through mail-order companies. However, you can make the following varieties of pasta using basic kitchen utensils.

Fettuccine and noodles: After rolling dough and letting it stand, cut into ¼-inch-wide strips. Shake the strands to separate. For thin noodles, cut into 2-inch lengths.

Linguine or tagliatelle: After rolling dough and letting it stand, cut into ⅛-inch-wide slices for linguine or ½-inch-wide slices for tagliatelle. Shake the strands to separate. For noodles, cut into 2-inch lengths.

Bow tie: Cut dough into 2 x 1–inch rectangles. Pinch the centers to form bow tie shape.

How to Cook Pasta

The secret to cooking pasta is to use enough water and to keep the water on a rolling boil all the way through cooking. Each pound of pasta requires 6 quarts of water, 1 teaspoon salt, and 1 tablespoon of vegetable oil. One pound of pasta makes four servings.

Cooking pasta: Bring water, salt, and oil to a rolling boil in a large, lidded pot. The oil prevents pasta from sticking together. Add one pound of pasta all at once. Cook fresh pasta for about 4 minutes, uncovered. Remove a piece near the end of cooking time and taste to determine if it is fully cooked. Most people prefer pasta cooked al dente (tender but firm), but this varies with taste. Keep pasta from sticking to bottom of pot while boiling by stirring occasionally.

Pasta Ideas

If you find that you enjoy making your own pasta from scratch, you may want to invest in a pasta press or machine, which will allow you to make many varieties of fresh pasta quickly and easily.

The variations of pasta run from A to Z! Here are some pasta forms that can be made with the right equipment:

acini di pepe, alphabets, bean threads, bow ties, capellini, cavatelli, couscous, ditalini, egg roll wrappers, fettuccine, gemelli, kluski, lasagne, linguine, macaroni, mafalda, manicotti, mostaccioli, noodles, orzo, ravioli, rice sticks, rigatoni, rings, rotini, shells, spaetzle, spaghetti, stars, tortellini, vermicelli, wagon wheels, wonton skins, ziti

Desserts

The Final Show

Dessert is the perfect conclusion to a meal. When preparing your desserts, think of appealing to all the senses. Desserts can be served simply, with just a touch of decoration, or can be molded and decorated into elegant works of art.

Visual appeal is always important to the presentation of dessert, for it is the last dish your guests will see.

Dessert garnish suggestions: mint sprigs, chopped nuts, whipped cream, sour cream, cream cheese, yogurt, cookie crumbs, crushed candy, and shaved chocolate.

Double-Boiler Cooking

This method is used often when creating desserts, whenever an indirect, gentle heat is needed. A double boiler consists of two pans, which can be metal, glass, or ceramic; one fits on top of the other. The bottom pan contains water and the top pan sits over (not in) the water.

Gallery of Sauces for Dessert Presentations

Dessert Painting

Dessert painting relies on contrasting colors, a steady hand, and a very finely pointed knife or wooden toothpick.

To practice, pour a couple of tablespoons of chocolate syrup on one side of each plate. Using a squeeze bottle or paper funnel, pipe a spiral of custard sauce on top. Make designs by drawing the point of a sharp knife or wooden pick through the custard sauce. Try some of the following designs:

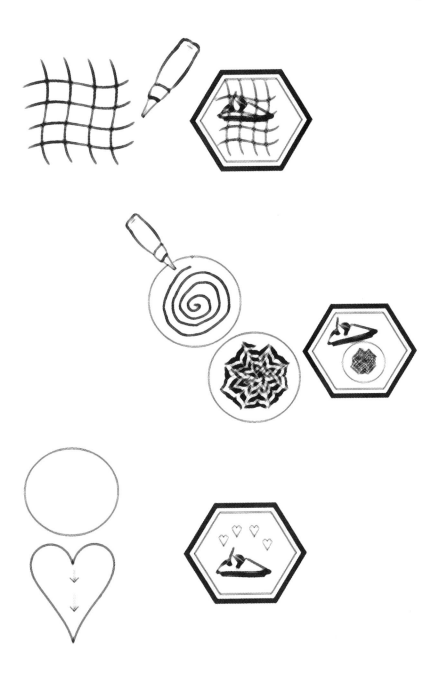

You can also make spiderweb design by drawing the point of a sharp knife or wooden pick into the middle, then out at a different angle of custard with a spiral of chocolate sauce.

Custard Sauce

This sauce gives a perfect off-white/yellow base for a dark sauce topping.

3   EGG *yolks*
1   *cup* HEAVY CREAM
¼   *cup* CONFECTIONERS' SUGAR, *sifted*
1   *teaspoon* VANILLA EXTRACT

In a small, heavy double boiler, combine egg yolks, heavy cream, sugar, and vanilla. Whisk constantly until mixture is creamy and thick enough that the whisk leaves a visible trail on the bottom of the pan. While cooking, be careful not to let mixture overheat, otherwise, the egg yolks will curdle. Remove mixture from heat and cool, stirring occasionally. Strain. Pour sauce on plate and spread. Garnish with Kahlúa Chocolate Sauce (see page 151) or fruit purée.

Yield: 1½ cups

Papaya and Raspberry Purées

Puréed fruit makes a nice touch. This sauce will add color and flavor to many desserts.

Papaya Purée
1   *medium* PAPAYA, *ripe*
2   *tablespoons* CONFECTIONERS' SUGAR, *sifted*

Raspberry Purée
1   *pint* RASPBERRIES, *washed*
2   *tablespoons* CONFECTIONERS' SUGAR, *sifted*

Peel and deseed papaya. Wash raspberries. In a food processor, purée fruit to a smooth paste, pausing twice to scrape down sides of bowl. Keep the two purées separate.

Place Papaya Purée in a small saucepan over moderate heat. Add powdered sugar and cook 3–5 minutes. If needed, add arrowroot or cornstarch to thicken. Strain fruit into a bowl through a fine sieve to remove seeds and fiber. Purée should be smooth. Repeat cooking and straining process with Raspberry Purée. Cool before serving.

Yield: 1+ cup each

Rose Melba

Melba is a pinkish, thickened combination of raspberries, currant jelly, and sugar.

½   *cup store-bought* RASPBERRY MELBA SAUCE
¼   *cup plain* YOGURT

Mix melba and yogurt well. Strain thoroughly and refrigerate. When ready to use, place in a plastic squeeze bottle and dribble on plates to create designs.

Yield: ¾ cup

Kahlúa Chocolate Sauce

A chocolate sauce delicately flavored with a coffee liqueur from Mexico.

1   *8-ounce package* SEMISWEET CHOCOLATE BITS
1   *tablespoon* LIGHT CORN SYRUP
2   *tablespoons* LIGHT CREAM
½   *tablespoon* BOILING WATER *or* HOT COFFEE
½   *teaspoon* VANILLA EXTRACT
2   *teaspoons* KAHLÚA LIQUEUR

Melt chocolate in double boiler. Add corn syrup, stir, and slowly add cream. Stir until mixture is smooth and cook for 15 to 20 minutes. If the mixture is too thick, add coffee or water. Add vanilla extract and remove from heat. Mix Kahlúa well with chocolate sauce. Place in refrigerator until ready to use. When ready to use, reheat in double boiler and, while warm, place in ketchup bottle and dribble on plates to create designs.

Yield: 1+ cup

Whipped Cream

Make your own whipped cream. It makes a great topping for many desserts.

½   *cup* HEAVY WHIPPING CREAM
3   *tablespoons* CONFECTIONERS' SUGAR
2   *teaspoons* VANILLA EXTRACT

Using a wire whisk or electric mixer, beat heavy cream in a mixing bowl set on top of another mixing bowl containing ice cubes (this will help the cream to form into peaks), just until cream thickens. When peaks start to form, add sugar and vanilla. Then whip to the desired consistency.

Yield: 2 cups

Recipes

Baked Florida Grapefruit

Grapefruit is a citrus fruit grown in abundance in Florida and other regions.

1		GRAPEFRUIT
½	*cup*	GRANULATED SUGAR
2	*tablespoons*	CRÈME DE MENTHE *or* SHERRY
2	*scoops*	VANILLA ICE CREAM
2	*tablespoons*	PECANS, *chopped*

Cut grapefruit in half crosswise, remove seeds and loosen fruit from skin. Sprinkle surface with sugar and drizzle with liqueur. In oven, under preheated broiler, broil until sugar starts to caramelize. Remove grapefruit from oven and top with ice cream and pecans.

Yield: 2 servings

Exotic Rum-Grilled Fruit Kabobs

A fun and enjoyable way to get your guests involved in the making of the dessert.

1		STAR FRUIT *(carambola), cubed*
¼		PAPAYA, *peeled and cubed*
¼		PINEAPPLE, *peeled and cubed*
1	*cup*	DARK RUM
½	*cup*	BROWN SUGAR
1		*dozen wooden skewers, 8 to 10 inches in length*

Combine star fruit, papaya, and pineapple cubes in a flat bowl. Add rum and cover with plastic wrap, chill for 1 to 2 hours.

In separate bowls, place fruit and brown sugar. Put on a table next to the grill with bamboo skewers. Have each guest spear pieces of fruit, roll them in brown sugar, and hold over grill until surface glazes and lightly browns. Cool slightly before eating.

Yield: 2 servings

Coconut Grove Papaya Custard

For this dessert, you will make a molded custard and then bake it to perfection.

Preheat oven to 350°F.

2	*tablespoons* TOASTED COCONUT
1	*cup* HEAVY CREAM
1	*tablespoon* VANILLA EXTRACT
2	EGG YOLKS
1	*whole* EGG
3	*tablespoons* CONFECTIONERS' SUGAR
1	*tablespoon* GRAND MARNIER *or* RUM

Papaya Purée (see page 150)

Garnish

MINT LEAVES

Make Papaya Purée Sauce and set aside.

Toast coconut in 350°F oven. Scald cream in saucepan over moderate heat. In mixing bowl, beat coconut, vanilla, eggs, sugar, and Grand Marnier. Pour in scalded heavy cream while beating. Pour mixture into custard dishes. Set filled custard dishes in a shallow pan of hot water and place in oven. Bake at 350°F for 35 minutes or until knife inserted near center comes out clean. Cool.

When cool, loosen the custard from dishes by lightly heating bottom of dish. Use hot paring knife to cut around edges, then invert on plates. Dribble Papaya Purée over custard and garnish with mint leaves.

Yield: 2 servings

Double-Layered Strawberry Shortcake

American shortcake is a large, sweet biscuit that is split in half, then filled and topped with sliced strawberries. This recipe makes shortcake just like Grandma used to make it. She will love you for cooking the old-fashioned way.

Preheat oven to 450°F

½	*pint* STRAWBERRIES
½	*cup* WATER
2	*tablespoons* GRANULATED SUGAR
2	*cups* WHIPPED CREAM (*see page 151*)

Shortcake Dough

| 1 | *cup all-purpose* FLOUR |
| 1 | *teaspoon double-acting* BAKING POWDER |

¼	teaspoon BAKING SODA
1/4	teaspoon SALT
3	tablespoons GRANULATED SUGAR
2	tablespoons BUTTER *or* MARGARINE
1	EGG WHITE
6	tablespoons MILK
¼	teaspoon ALMOND EXTRACT

To make Shortcake Dough, sift flour before measuring. In a mixing bowl, add flour, baking powder, baking soda, salt, and sugar. Next, cut butter into dry mixture with a pastry blender until it reaches consistency of coarse cornmeal. In a separate bowl, beat egg white, milk, and almond extract, add to flour mixture. Stir until the dough is fairly free from the sides of the bowl. On a lightly floured surface, knead dough (following How to Knead directions on page 143). Roll out to ½-inch thickness. Form two biscuits. Place biscuits on baking sheet sprayed with nonstick spray. Bake at 450°F for 15 to 20 minutes or until lightly browned on top. In center, insert knife. If it comes out clean, dough is done. Cool. Split shortcake in half crosswise and set aside.

Wash and clean strawberries, pick off the stems, and slice. Place in small mixing bowl and add water and sugar, mixing thoroughly. Let sit 20 minutes before using.

On two plates, place bottoms of cut shortcake, cover with half of strawberries and sauce. Place small amount of Whipped Cream on top. Place other half of shortcake on top and pour on remaining strawberry sauce, finish with a heaping spoonful of Whipped Cream on top and sides. Serve immediately.

Yield: 2 servings

Homemade Bread Pudding with Brandy Sauce
A south Florida dessert favorite.

Preheat oven to 375°F.

4	slices of BREAD
1	cup MILK
2	large EGGS
¾	cup SUGAR
¼	cup RAISINS

1   *tablespoon* VANILLA EXTRACT
½   *tablespoon* CINNAMON
½   *cup canned* FRUIT COCKTAIL, *drained*
2   *tablespoons* MELTED BUTTER

Brandy Sauce

2   *large* EGGS
¼   *cup* GRANULATED SUGAR
2   *tablespoons* MELTED BUTTER
½   *cup* HEAVY CREAM
1   *teaspoon* VANILLA EXTRACT
¼   *cup* BRANDY

Grease pan with 1 tablespoon melted butter. Mix bread, milk, eggs, sugar, raisins, vanilla extract, cinnamon, and drained fruit cocktail. Pour into pan and bake at 375°F for 15 minutes. Remove dough from oven, brush with 1 tablespoon melted butter, and place back in oven, 20 to 25 more minutes or until knife inserted pulls out clean. Top with brandy sauce.

To prepare Brandy Sauce, in top pan of double boiler (with about a quart of water in the bottom), combine eggs, sugar, melted butter, milk, and vanilla extract. Beat until eggs foam on top. Place double boiler on medium heat. Stir constantly until thickened to the consistency of soft pudding. When mixture is thick enough, stir in brandy. Cook and stir 1 more minute, then remove from heat. Place in refrigerator until ready to serve.

Yield: 4 servings

Key Lime Torte with Graham Cracker Topping

This recipe is a favorite of mine. Key lime in a torte shell and smothered with graham cracker crust—wow!

Preheat oven to 350°F.

2   *large* EGGS
2   *large* EGG YOLKS
½   *cup* CONFECTIONERS' SUGAR
½   *cup* KEY LIME JUICE
½   *cup* SWEETENED CONDENSED MILK
1   *teaspoon* LIME RIND, *grated*

4   *tablespoons* UNSALTED BUTTER
½   *teaspoon* CREAM OF TARTAR
1   *tablespoon* MELTED BUTTER
1   *cup* GRAHAM CRACKER *crumbs*

Torte Dough

2¼   *cups* FLOUR
⅛   *teaspoon* SALT
¾   *cup* CONFECTIONERS' SUGAR, *sifted*
2   *large* EGGS
7   *tablespoons* COLD UNSALTED BUTTER
1   *baking pan flan ring, 8½ inches in diameter*

To make Torte Dough, sift flour before measuring. Place flour on work surface and make a well in the center. Cut the butter into small pieces and place in the middle of the flour, work with your fingertips until butter is softened. Add sugar and salt, mix thoroughly, then add the eggs and mix. Gradually add the flour into the mixture. Blend until thoroughly mixed. When done, work the dough in the palm of your hand until it is smooth. Roll dough into a ball, cover with plastic wrap, and refrigerate for several hours.

On a lightly floured surface, roll out the refrigerated pastry dough into a circle, about ⅛-inch thick. Lightly grease the flan ring, then line it with pastry dough. Using your fingertips, lightly pinch the edges of the pastry to form a little crest. Bake at 350°F for 30 minutes. Once it is cooled, remove the ring.

To prepare the key lime mix, in a double boiler (following Double-Boiler Cooking instructions on page 148), place whole eggs, egg yolks, sugar, lime juice, milk, cream of tartar, and lime rind. Place bowl over pan of boiling water and whisk until mixture thickens to the consistency of mayonnaise. Remove from heat, whisk in 4 tablespoons unsalted butter, 2 tablespoons at a time. Pour into cooked torte shell. Thoroughly mix graham crackers with melted butter and sprinkle on top. Refrigerate for 2 hours before serving.

Yield: 1 pie

Mango Bavarian Cream

Bavarian cream is a stirred custard lightened with whipped cream and set with gelatin. In this recipe, it will be seasoned with ripe, sweet mango purée.

½   VANILLA BEAN, *split*

½   *cup* MILK

2   *large* EGG YOLKS

6   *tablespoons* CONFECTIONERS' SUGAR

½   *cup* MANGO, *puréed*

1   *envelope* UNFLAVORED GELATIN, *softened in 2 tablespoons cold water*

1   *cup* WHIPPED CREAM *(see page 151)*

2   *sprigs* MINT LEAVES

In saucepan over moderate heat, combine vanilla bean and milk and cook until bubbles form around edge. Set to the side.

In a medium mixing bowl, combine egg yolks and sugar and blend thoroughly. Remove vanilla bean from milk and gradually pour hot milk into mixing bowl, constantly whipping with a whisk. In a separate bowl, mix gelatin and water until soft. Add softened gelatin and mango purée to mix. Heat until gelatin is dissolved, about 6 to 7 minutes, over moderate-low heat, stirring constantly to keep egg from scrambling. Cool and refrigerate until almost set. In a mixing bowl, using a wire whisk or electric whip, beat heavy cream until stiff peaks form. Fold Whipped Cream into chilled mixture. Place in serving glasses. Refrigerate 3 to 4 hours or until firm. Garnish with mint leaves.

Yield: 2 servings

Orange Grove Sorbet

"Sorbet" is the French word for sherbet, which the Italians call sorbetto.

3   *cups* ORANGE JUICE

½   *cup* CONFECTIONERS' SUGAR, *sifted*

ORANGE SLICES *for garnish*

In mixing bowl, place juice and sugar, stir until sugar is dissolved. Freeze for 3 hours, removing the bowl from the freezer three times to stir during freezing. If mix is solidly frozen, break up with a flat knife. Spoon mixture into a food processor and blend until light and fluffy. Remove from processor and serve in a bowl garnished with orange slices. The sorbet can be kept in the freezer until ready to serve.

Yield: 3 cups

Pecan Sand Tarts

This is a cookie that you will love.

Preheat oven to 350°F.

½	*cup* BUTTER *or* MARGARINE
2	*tablespoons* CONFECTIONERS' SUGAR
1	*tablespoon* VANILLA EXTRACT
1	*cup all-purpose* FLOUR
¾	*teaspoon* BAKING POWDER
¼	*teaspoon* SALT
¼	*cup* PECANS, *chopped fine*

Mix butter, sugar, and vanilla and set aside. Sift together flour, baking powder, and salt. Gradually add flour mixture to creamed butter, then mix in nuts. Roll into 1-inch balls and drop onto greased cookie sheet. Lightly mash each ball slightly flat. Bake at 350°F for 15 to 20 minutes. If desired, roll in powdered sugar when cooled.

Yield: 8 Sand Tarts

Vanilla Ice Cream Crepes with Strawberry Sauce

Crepes are tissue-thin pancakes that can be used to make any number of delicious desserts. In this recipe, you will fill crepes with ice cream and smother with Strawberry Sauce and whipped cream.

1	*pint* STRAWBERRIES, *washed*
6	*tablespoons* WATER
2	*tablespoons* GRANULATED SUGAR
3	*cups* VANILLA ICE CREAM
4	*cups* WHIPPED CREAM *(see page 151)*

Crepe Shells

¼	*cup all-purpose* FLOUR
7	*tablespoons* MILK
1	*large* EGG
½	*tablespoon* VEGETABLE OIL
1	*pinch* SALT
	vegetable spray or oil

Combine flour, milk, egg, oil, and salt in a blender or food processor. Blend into a smooth batter, stopping motor a few times to scrape down the sides of the bowl. Cover and refrigerate batter for 1 hour. Blend batter well before making crepes.

Over moderate heat, lightly oil a preheated, 6-inch, nonstick sauté pan. Add enough batter to make a thin coat, tilt pan so batter forms a thin, even covering over bottom of sauté pan. Cook each crepe until it sets, about 45 seconds, flip over and cook other side for 30 seconds.

Place cooked crepe on waxed paper or clean, dry surface. Do not stack crepes while hot. Cooled crepes may be stacked, wrapped in aluminum foil, and refrigerated for a few days or frozen for a few months. If frozen, thaw in refrigerator for 6 hours before use.

Pick stems off strawberries and slice; place in mixing bowl with sugar and water. Lay crepes out flat and place a scoop of ice cream in middle. Roll up crepes and place on plates. Smother with strawberries and sauce. Garnish with whipped cream and serve immediately.

Yield: 4 servings

Wild Berry and Star Fruit Compote
Slow cooking is important for the fruit to retain its shape.

3	*cups mixed* BLACKBERRIES, RASPBERRIES, STRAWBERRIES, *and* BLUEBERRIES
½	*cup* ORANGE JUICE
½	*cup* CONFECTIONERS' SUGAR, *sifted*
1	*tablespoon quick-cooking* TAPIOCA
1	STAR FRUIT (CARAMBOLA), *sliced four times cross-wise to form stars*
2	*scoops* VANILLA ICE CREAM
2	*sprigs* MINT LEAVES

Rinse fruit. Place berries, orange juice, and sugar in a saucepan and bring to a simmer over moderate heat. Reduce heat and simmer for 5 minutes. Using a strainer, remove fruit from saucepan and place in a dish. Set to the side. Stir tapioca into the liquid left in the saucepan and simmer for 4 to 5 minutes, stirring occasionally. Add berries and star fruit to saucepan and remove from heat. Let sit for 20 minutes.

On two large plates, place ice cream and pour fruit compote over top. Garnish with mint leaves and serve immediately.

Yield: 2 servings

Lemon Sponge

A nice dessert that makes a perfectly light, yet filling, finish!

Preheat oven to 325°F.

1½	tablespoons all-purpose FLOUR
½	cup SUGAR
	pinch of SALT
1	large EGG, *separated*
1	teaspoon grated LEMON PEEL
1	tablespoon LEMON JUICE
½	tablespoon BUTTER, *melted*
½	cup MILK
	ROSE MELBA *(see page 150)*
	CUSTARD SAUCE *(see page 150)*

Prepare Rose Melba and Custard Sauce. Set aside.

Boil one quart of water. Mix flour, sugar, and salt together and set to the side. In another bowl, slightly beat egg yolk and add lemon peel, lemon juice, and butter. Stir in milk and flour mixture and set to the side.

Beat egg whites at high speed until soft peaks form when the beaters are slowly raised. Fold lemon mix into beaten egg white with a wire whisk or rubber spatula. Pour mixture into two or three custard cups. Set cups in a deep baking pan filled with boiling water (the water should be at the same level as the mixture in the cups). Cover pan and bake at 325°F for 40 minutes, or until lemon sponges are firm. Allow to cool and place in refrigerator to set. Once set, loosen lemon sponges from cups using a knife and plop them upside down onto plates. Dribble portions with Custard Sauce and Rose Melba. Serve immediately.

Yield: 2 servings

Glossary

Antipasto	A first course of assorted relishes and seafood
Bake	To cook covered or uncovered in an oven or oven-type appliance
Beat	To add air to a mixture with a brisk whipping or stirring motion using a spoon or electric mixer
Béchamel	A rich, white cream sauce
Blanch	To precook in boiling water or steam
Blend	To thoroughly mix two ingredients
Boil	To cook in a liquid at the boiling point (212°F) while bubbles rise to the top
Bread	To coat with bread crumbs before cooking
Chill	To place in refrigerator to reduce temperature
Chop	To cut into pea-sized pieces
Coulis	A sauce made from ingredients that have been pureed and strained
Crouton	A small cube of toasted bread served atop soup or salad
Cut in	To mix shortening with dry ingredients using a pastry blender, knives, or food processor
Dice	To cut food into small cubes
Dissolve	To disperse a dry substance in a liquid to form a solution
Dredge	To sprinkle or coat with flour or other fine substance
Egg wash	Whole egg, egg white, or egg yolk mixed with a small amount of water or milk
Fillet	A strip of fish without bone
Flake	To break lightly into small pieces
Fold	To gently add ingredients to a mixture using a spatula

Française	Coated with egg, Parmesan, and chopped parsley, then sautéed and served with lemon butter sauce
French knife:	Knife for chopping with a heavy 8-inch blade tapered to a slight point. Also known as a chef's knife
Fry	To cook in hot grease or shortening. Pan frying uses a small amount of fat; deep frying uses a large amount
Garnish	To trim a meal or plate with small pieces of colorful food
Glaze	A mixture applied to food that hardens or becomes firm and adds a glossy appearance
Julienne	Matchlike strips of vegetables or fruits
Marinate	To allow a food to soak in a liquid to tenderize or to add flavor
Mince	To chop food into very small pieces
Mirepoix	A mixture of roughly cut or diced vegetables, spices, and herbs used for flavoring
Mix	To combine ingredients, usually by stirring, till evenly distributed
Mornay	A cheese-flavored white sauce
Parboil	To cook partially in a boiling or simmering liquid
Poach	To cook in a hot liquid (160°F–180°F), ensuring that the food holds its shape while cooking
Precook	To cook food partially or completely before final cooking or preheating
Puree	A paste or thick liquid made from food
Reduce	To cook by simmering or boiling until a certain quantity of liquid is decreased; usually done to concentrate flavors
Roux	A mixture of flour and fat that is cooked and used to thicken soups and sauces
Sauté	To brown or cook in a small amount of hot shortening or oil
Simmer	To cook in liquid over low heat (185°F–210°F)
Stir	To mix ingredients with a circular motion until well blended
Whip	To incorporate air into a mixture by beating rapidly

Index

If you enjoyed this book, here are some other Pineapple Press titles you might enjoy as well. To request our complete catalog or to place an order, write to Pineapple Press, P.O. Box 3899, Sarasota, Florida 34230, or call 1-800-PINEAPL (746-3275). Or visit our website at www.pineapplepress.com.

The Everglades: River of Grass, 50th Anniversary Edition by Marjory Stoneman Douglas. This is the treasured classic of nature writing, first published fifty years ago, that captured attention all over the world and launched the fight to save the Everglades. The 50th Anniversary Edition includes an update on the events in the Glades in the last ten years. ISBN 1-56164-135-9 (hb)

Growing Family Fruit and Nut Trees by Marian Van Atta. How to enjoy all phases of growing your own delicious fruits, nuts, vegetables, herbs, and wild edibles. Includes planting and growing instructions as well as recipes for enjoying your bountiful crops. ISBN 1-56164-001-8 (pb)

Guide to Florida Lighthouses by Elinor De Wire. Its lighthouses are some of Florida's oldest and most historic structures, with diverse styles of architecture and daymark designs. ISBN 0-910923-74-4 (pb)

Guide to the Gardens of Florida by Lilly Pinkas. Organized by region, this guide provides detailed information on the featured species and facilities offered by Florida's public gardens. Includes 16 pages of color photos and 40 line drawings. ISBN 1-56164-169-3

The Mostly Mullet Cookbook by George "Grif" Griffin. Mulletheads unite! Includes dozens of mullet main dishes, such as Dixie Fried Mullet, Mullet Italiano, Sweet & Sour Mullet, and the Sea Dog Sandwich, as well as mullet-friendly sides and sauces and other great Southern seafood, including Judy's Mullet Butter and Ybor City Street Vendor's Crab Cakes. ISBN 1-56164-147-2 (pb)

The Sunshine State Almanac and Book of Florida-Related Stuff by Phil Philcox and Beverly Boe. Chock-full of statistics, recipes, and photos, this handy reference is a veritable cornucopia of helpful and just plain fascinating stuff! Includes a long list of what's going on around Florida every month of the year. ISBN 1-56164-178-2 (pb)

Visiting Small-Town Florida Volumes 1 and 2 by Bruce Hunt. Filled with both color and black-and-white photos, these two guidebooks will have you exploring the Florida that used to be. Visit charming inns, antique shops, and historic homes, and sample authentic home cooking along the way! Volume 1: ISBN 1-56164-128-6 (pb); Volume 2: ISBN 1-56164-180-4 (pb)